Handy Guide
Victoria Falls

PAUL TINGAY & DOUG SCOTT

Struik Publishers (Pty) Ltd
(a member of The Struik Publishing
Group (Pty) Ltd)
80 McKenzie Street, Cape Town 8001

Reg. No.: 54/00965/07

First published in 1996

Copyright © 1996 in published edition:
Struik Publishers (Pty) Ltd
Copyright © 1996 in text: Paul Tingay
and Doug Scott
Copyright © 1996 in photography: as
credited on this page
Copyright © 1996 in maps: Globetrotter
Travel Maps

Managing editor: Annlerie van Rooyen
Editor: Glynne Williamson
Design and DTP: Darren MacGurk
Cover design: Darren MacGurk
Design manager: Petal Palmer
DTP maps: Karen Bailey

Reproduction by Unifoto (Pty) Ltd,
Cape Town
Printed and bound by Tien Wah Press
(Pte.) Ltd, Singapore

All rights reserved. No part of this
publication may be reproduced, stored
in a retrieval system, or transmitted in
any form or by any means, electronic,
mechanical, photocopying, recording
or otherwise, without the prior written
permission of the copyright owners.

ISBN 1 86825 891 2

Every effort has been made to ensure
factual accuracy in this book, but with
the rapid changes taking place in Zimbabwe, it is inevitable that information
will become outdated. The authors and
publishers invite any comments for future
updates. Write to: The Editor, Handy
Guide Victoria Falls, Struik Publishers,
P O Box 1144, Cape Town 8000.

The authors and publishers would like to
thank the following persons for their
invaluable assistance:
Jeremy Brooke of Shearwater Adventures
Lance Reynolds of Europcar
Ann Smythe of Zimbabwe Sun Hotels
Sarah-Jayne Lightfoot

PHOTOGRAPHIC CREDITS

Copyright rests with the photographers and/or their agents as listed below.
PA = Photo Access   SIL = Struik Image Library
Brett, M. pp. 22; 47; 49; **Bristow, D.** p. 48 [PA] **Cubitt, G.** pp. 6; 15 bottom; 21; 28; 30/31; 37 **de la Harpe, R.** front and back cover [SIL]; pp. 10/11 [SIL]; 12 [SIL]; 14; 16; 18 top [SIL]; 19 [SIL]; 20 [SIL]; 23 [SIL]; 24 [SIL]; 26 [SIL]; 33 [SIL]; 36 [SIL]; 38 [SIL]; 43 [SIL]; 52 [SIL]; 53 [SIL]; 55 [SIL] **Dennis, N.** p. 27; 29 [SIL]; 39 **Knirr, W.** p. 45 **Paterson-Jones, C.** pp. 15 top; 41 **Skinner, M.** [all SIL] pp. 13; 18 bottom; 35; 40; 57 bottom; 58; 59 **Tingay, P.** pp. 25; 56; 57 top **Wagner, P.** [both PA] pp. 32; 34

FOREWORD FROM AGFA

AGFA are delighted to join forces with Struik Publishers in bringing the **Handy Guide Victoria Falls** to the shelves.

Along with camera and film, this guide will prove to be an invaluable companion to all travellers. Illustrated throughout with beautiful, full-colour photographs, this compact book is an ideal way to get acquainted with your chosen destination.

The handy photo and travel tips, along with clear, easy-to-follow maps, will help you make the most of your visit.

And when your holiday is over, bring your memories home on AGFA film. You can depend on our widely available range of HDC print film or RSX and CTX slide film to capture the beauty of your holiday in High Definition Colour.

KEY TO SYMBOLS

- 🚶 **WALKS, HIKES AND TRAILS**
- 🐦 **BIRDLIFE**
- 🏛 **MUSEUMS/MONUMENTS/ GALLERIES**
- 📷 **PHOTO TIPS**
- ✟ **WILDLIFE, NATIONAL PARKS, GAME PARKS/RESERVES**
- 👫 **ENTERTAINMENT/ EXCURSIONS/LEISURE**
- 🗺 **OF HISTORIC/CULTURAL INTEREST**
- ❀ **FLORA/BOTANICAL PARKS AND RESERVES**
- 🐎 **HORSE-RIDING/PONY TREKKING/EQUESTRIAN SPORTS**
- ℹ **TOURIST INFORMATION**
- 🍴 **EATING AND DRINKING**
- 🎁 **SHOPPING**
- 🚂 **TRAIN TRIPS/RAILWAY MUSEUMS**
- 🏃 **SPORTS**
- 🛏 **ACCOMMODATION**

CONTENTS

Introduction 4

The Falls 6

The Rain Forest 14

The Town 16

Around and about Victoria Falls 26

The River 30

Excursions 38

Visitor's Digest 60

Index 64

INTRODUCTION

 WATERFALLS
* **Victoria Falls:** Greatest grandstand of falling water
* **Largest falls: Bridal Veil Falls,** California
* **Highest falls: Angel Falls,** Venezuela, at 979 m (3,212 ft)
* **Greatest flow: Guaira Falls,** Paraguay/Brazil
* **Widest falls: Khone Falls,** Laos, at 11 km (7 miles)
* **Niagara Falls:** Best known after Victoria Falls

 TOP SPOTS AT VICTORIA FALLS
Devil's Cataract, the **Rain Forest, Main Falls, Victoria Falls Bridge** to bungi-jump, the **Batoka Gorge** on a white-water raft, canoeing or cruising **the Zambezi,** the **Victoria Falls Hotel** and traditional dancing at the **Falls Craft Village.**

 AGFA PHOTO TIP
Early in the morning, drive high up **Courteney Selous Crescent** and you will look right onto the boiling mist of the Falls with the rising sun glowing immediately behind it – a dazzling inferno shot.

Victoria Falls, *mosi-oa-tunya*, the smoke that thunders – and this massive, mile-wide, horizon-to-horizon waterfall really does thunder. Rock solid ground vibrates to the roar of 500,000 m³ (14,158 ft³) of water per minute, hurtling in a wide-angle fury of churning, green-white water a mere 60 m (200 ft) away from the Rain Forest. Often called the greatest tapestry of falling water in the world, its apocalyptic symphony of water, rock and updraughts whipped into mist clouds 300 m (1,000 ft) high, create shadows and rainbows across the chasm.

Victoria Falls is also a romance of vintage steam trains, an Edwardian Raj hotel with colonial white-gloved service, old-fashioned river adventure, of canoeing and kayaking through the rapids of the lush ilala palm and baobab jungle of the upper Zambezi, traditional African dancing, and of the exhilarating river rodeo of white-water rafting in the steep-sided gorges below the Falls.

The twin-pontoon seaplane that skims the surface of the smooth-flowing Zambezi, imitating the old flying boats that used to lake-hop the Rift Valley down an entire

continent to Cape Town, adds to the air of nostalgia. Also on offer are microlight flights, bungi-jumping, golf, horse riding, fishing and superb big game viewing.

The town itself is tiny though crammed full with rafters, safari vehicles, bicyclists and backpackers. It lies alongside the Victoria Falls National Park and wild animals, although not frequent, move freely through the area, especially after dark. Luxury thatched safari lodges inland and on the river offer water hole game-viewing.

HISTORY

Man has lived in the vicinity of the Victoria Falls and its gorges for thousands of years. Many of his cleverly chipped stones and scrapers have been found by scientists along the gorges. In more modern times, first the hunter-gatherers were here, followed by the Tonga, Lozi, Kololo and Leya, part of Zimbabwe's ruling Rozvi 200 years ago. Then came the Ndebele impis from the south and 30 years later, in 1855, the first of the white men.

Some will speculate that the Portuguese explorer and ivory trader, Antonio da Silvo Porto, and a Hungarian, Laszlo Magyar, may possibly have seen the Falls before Livingstone, while hunter-trader James Chapman had been very near them in 1853. Certainly their existence was known in South Africa from about 1840. Livingstone paid two visits to the Falls, one in 1855 and another in 1860. Artist Thomas Baines went there in 1862 and by 1870, 25 Westerners had visited the Falls, including legendary hunter Frederick Courteney Selous who described it as 'one of the most transcendentally beautiful natural phenomena on this side of paradise'. The first permanent European settler was F.J. 'Mopane' Clarke in 1898, trader, pub-owner and forwarding agent at the malaria-ridden Old Drift 9 km (5.5 miles) upstream of the Falls. Gambling and drinking were the two main activities in the old days at Clarke's bar.

In 1904 the town of Livingstone was formally established in Zambia and by March 1907, had two hotels, a restaurant, chemist and a barber. The railway and bridge were complete by 1905 and a tin-roofed Victoria Falls Hotel built. The Victoria Falls National Park was declared in 1951 and major tourism development on the Zimbabwean side began in the mid-1960s.

DR LIVINGSTONE, I PRESUME?
These are the famous words of **Sir Henry Morton Stanley**, sent by his newspaper, The New York Herald, to find **Dr Livingstone** presumed lost somewhere in Africa. He found him on 10 November 1871. Stanley led another three Africa expeditions and was responsible for Belgium obtaining its Congo colony. The highest peak in the Mountains of the Moon (dividing Uganda from Zaire), a waterfall, a town and a lake, all in Africa, were named after him.

THOMAS BAINES
Baines journeyed overland with hunter-trader James Chapman from Walvis Bay in Namibia through Botswana to the Victoria Falls, arriving there in 1862. Baines, self-taught, painted the most evocative and colourful oils of the Falls, especially of canoes, and also of buffalo grazing on the lip of the chasm. Many of his paintings are in the **National Archives**, Harare; reproductions can be seen in the **Victoria Falls Hotel** and copies are on sale. He painted 400 oils and as many water-colours.

THE FALLS

PHOTO TIP
The best shot of the Devil's Cataract can probably be taken at about 10h00 from one of the nearby vantage points in the Rain Forest. You will also get excellent views from the platform down the Chain Walk (at low water), which is just in front of Livingstone's statue, providing lovely silhouette foliage-frames of the chasm and where you will often see a double rainbow.

The Victoria Falls in northwest Zimbabwe is possibly Africa's premier. Approach it through the thatched archway entrance of the Victoria Falls National Park, then follow the paved walkway through the trees. The sequence of the Falls, beginning at Devil's Cataract, is Main Falls, Livingstone Island, Horseshoe Falls, Rainbow Falls and Danger Point, which overlooks the Boiling Pot in Zambia. You will find only a narrow wall of woven brush separating you from the bank at all these spots – remember that no-one has returned from an accidental journey down.

Devil's Cataract

From the air, the Zambezi is a green strip that twists and turns, fed by hundreds of tributaries. Upstream of the Falls, where only the chuckle of the Katombora rapids competes with the snorting of buffalo and

The turbulent Devil's Cataract hurls itself into the 100-m-deep (328 ft) chasm.

the bark of baboons, Africa's fourth largest river is a soft gold-green. You can stand at the water's edge beneath giant water berry trees and watch the gentle flow begin to shake off its lethargy and pick up speed.

Soon the race is on. The palm-lined shore seems to urge the great river on until, fretful and turbulent, it harnesses its massive strength, drops suddenly to the side of **Cataract Island** and in a slam-down, hurricane explosion of driving, frenzied suction, hurls itself over the basalt avalanche known as Devil's Cataract into the mist-churned chasm below.

Livingstone's statue

A huge bronze statue of Dr David Livingstone atop a plinth of chiselled granite reads 'Missionary, liberator, explorer'. It stares boldly across Devil's Cataract and was sculpted in 1933 by fellow Scot, Sir William Reid-Dick of London, as a tribute to 'a great Christian gentleman'.

Here, only a flimsy, metre-wide (40 inch) thorn barrier separates you from the Falls. The Devil's Cataract is the lowest of the five falls that make up the Victoria Falls and represents the place where the river is cutting a new channel and carving the next precipice over which, thousands of years hence, the Zambezi will fall. Go down the steep 73-step Chain Walk to the lower viewpoint cut into a niche of dripping rock and drenched jungle. Here the paradox of gentle bridal-veil spray meets the overwhelming fury of the Devil's wild, headlong plunge down rocks and tormented ravine.

'Missionary, liberator, explorer'.

 ISLAND ALOES
Lovely yellow-red aloes with their prickly spear-shaped leaves can often be seen growing in fault lines across the waterfall face of the wet basalt of **Cataract Island**. The word aloe originates from Arabic.

AIRPORT TAX
Zimbabwe has not yet had its airport departure tax incorporated into international tickets. Have US$20 available if leaving the country by air (Z$20 for residents). Tax of US$10 is also payable by non-Commonwealth members when crossing into Zambia.

 BELOVED PARTNER
'My dearie, my dearie, you are going to leave me. Are you resting on Jesus?' These were practically the last words **David Livingstone** spoke to his wife **Mary**, first-born child of missionaries **Robert and Mary Moffat** of Kuruman, as he beseeched his God and battled with all his medical knowledge to save her from malaria. She died on the morning of 27 April 1862 at Shupanga on the Zambezi and is buried in a lonely grave near the delta.

8 HANDY GUIDE VICTORIA FALLS

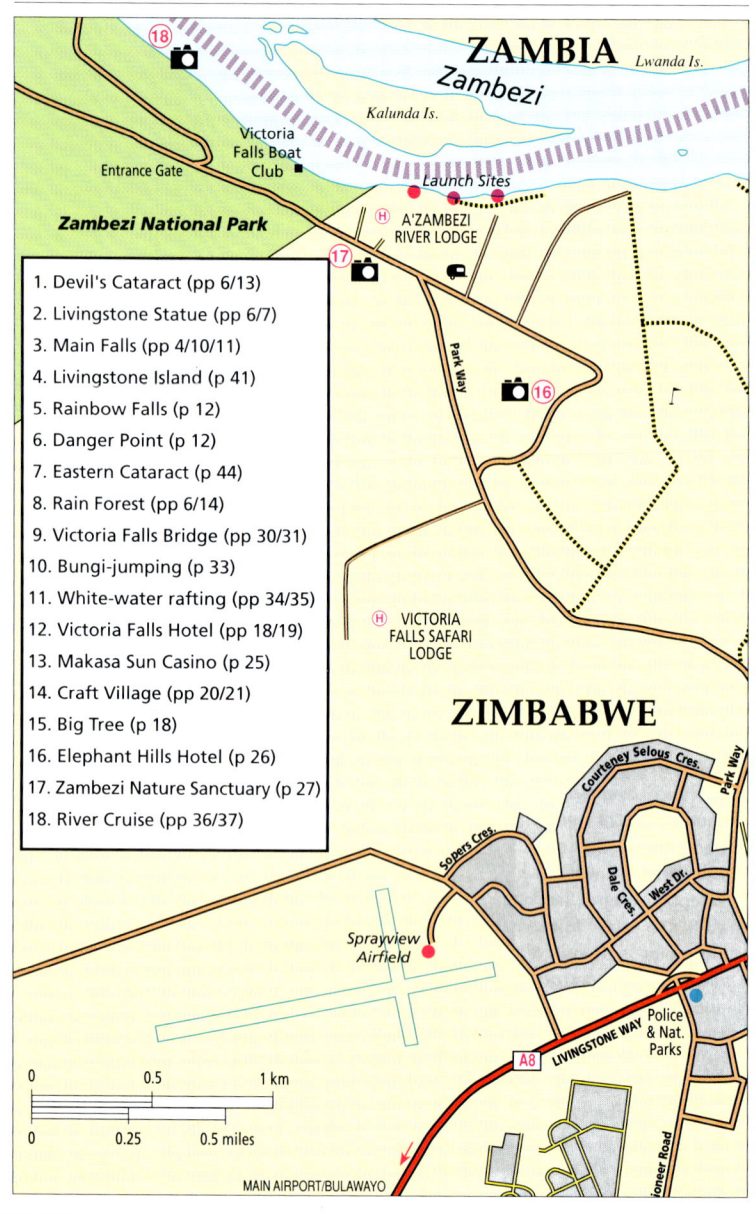

THE FALLS **9**

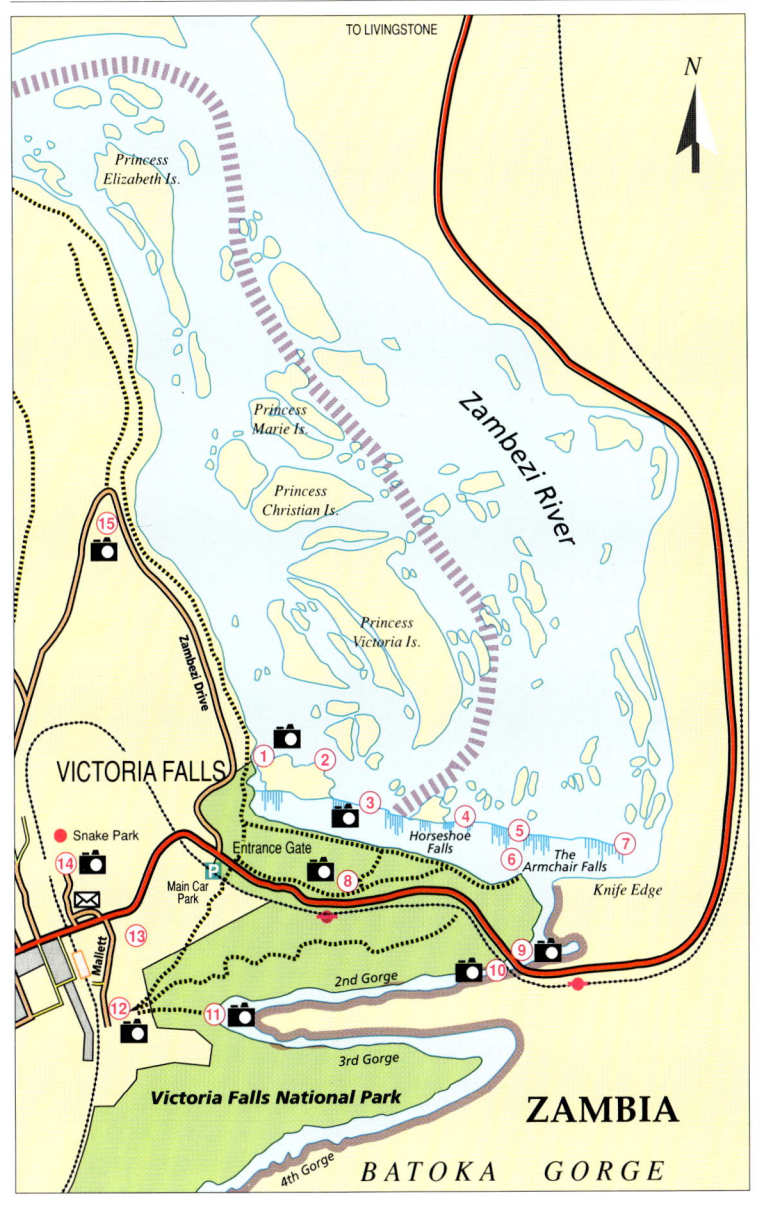

HANDY GUIDE VICTORIA FALLS

VICTORIA FALLS STATISTICS

* **Width:** 1 708 m (5 603 ft)
* **Height:** 100 m (328 ft)
* **Flow:** April: 500 million litres (100 million gallons) per minute
* **August:** 50 million litres (11 million gallons) per minute
* **October:** 22.5 million litres (5 million gallons) per minute

In 1958, nearly 50% more water flowed over the Falls after the floods than ever before recorded: 700,000 m³ (some 24,780,000 ft³) per minute.

UNCONVENTIONALLY TASTY

A treat in Matabeleland, including the Victoria Falls, is the **mopane caterpillar** which feeds on leaves from the mopane trees. It is coloured a dramatic yellow and green, and is rather frightening to look at with its spiky back. High in protein, the caterpillar forms part of the diet of many rural people. It is usually roasted over an open fire, and can be dried and stored for leaner days.

Main Falls, the world's greatest tapestry of falling water.

Main Falls

The great curtain of blinding white water drawn dramatically over black basalt seems to filter and comb the Zambezi into a silken frame. Up to 700,000 m³ (24,780,000 ft³) of water per minute has been known to thunder over the Falls, but at year's end it is only 3% of this. As the river dries, leaving Livingstone Island a green oasis, Main Falls is separated by expanses of baking basalt into smaller falls and silver cascades.

Take a raincoat to view the Falls, but keep your camera tucked away for your return trip. For the moment, simply enjoy the rainbow, sun-shot wonder and sheer majesty of it all, for the Falls is a place of many moods.

THE FALLS **11**

The avalanche is so noisy at times that you can't hear yourself, while the spray blows up at your feet, drenching those without coats in a retreat of laughter. The water falls 100 m (328 ft) into the gorge below you; it is not normally very deep here but it has been known to rise 18 m (59 ft) in times of flood, the sort of power and fury responsible for the zigzag gorges cut into the riverbed downstream.

Visit the Falls at full moon and see the ghostly lunar rainbow rising out of the dark chasm. It is an eerily beautiful sight as the spray drifts past the shadowed rain forest. Check with the National Park's wardens at the entrance to the Falls, or any tour operator as to the best times to visit, usually early morning or early evening.

SWIMMING POOLS
You'll find one at every hotel: the **Makasa Sun** pool is a lovely round creation near the breakfast patio, while the **A'Zambezi** pool is right on the riverbank – non-guests are welcome. Upriver young local boys, indifferent to crocs, swim in the Zambezi (a practice not recommended).

PHOTO TIP
You may need a polarizing filter to capture the sheer mirror of **Main Falls**, and some careful exposures for sunrise shots in winter when the sun comes up right behind Main Falls.

DRAGONFLIES
Being riverine, there are 100 species of dragon- and damselflies (Odonata) at Victoria Falls. The large, long-bodied emperor dragonfly can often be seen hovering over the waters, or zigzagging back and forth. There are also grasshoppers, stick insects, shore earwigs, termites, praying mantis, 80 species of butterfly, including swallowtails, and hundreds of different moths.

Seen from the Zambian side, the Falls is a magical display of spray and misty rainbows.

MOSI-OA-TUNYA *'The place of the rainbow' is one romantic interpretation of the Tokaleya, Batoka or now Tonga word* Shongwe, *meaning 'the fuming smoke'. Zulu-Ndebele impis called it* amanza thunquayo, *or 'water rising as smoke'. Livingstone was told it was* mo ku sa tunya musi, *'where there is always smoke rising'. He interpreted this as 'resounding smoke', and the 1878 missionary explorer, Francois Coillard, as today's* mosi-oa-tunya, *'the thundering smoke'.*

RAINBOW FALLS AND DANGER POINT

A path lined with weaver-nested wild date palms leads to the open basalt and spray-drenched platform of Danger Point. At low flood, it is dry, hot and in many ways the perfect vantage point to film the Falls.

Rainbow Falls

The path leading to Danger Point faces Rainbow Falls, and across the chasm you'll see rainbows that you don't often see: complete rainbows and double rainbows. Ahead of you will be people who can't see that they're standing in a rainbow, as the bright sun dazzles off the mist and wet rock around them.

Danger Point

Danger Point itself, where you appear to be on top of a 360° world of thundering water, is buried in spray when the river is flooding and the rocks then become perilously slick. Avoid going anywhere near the edge at this time. All the grass bends away from Danger

Point because of the wind and the great, drenching sheets of mist-rain that attack the umbrellas of visitors like angry squalls at sea. In the dry season you can get closer to the edge to see where the Zambezi makes good its escape into the second of the huge gorges of the Batoka. Right in front of the onslaught of cascading water, the so-called **Boiling Pot** seems deceptively calm, but there are powerful currents here that have pulled down several people who've tried to swim this close to the Falls. The route back from Danger Point runs closer to the railway line and the National Park's exit gate.

BIRD-WATCHING
Over 400 species of bird occur at the Victoria Falls and in the vicinity, ranging from the shoreline pelicans, sacred ibis, ducks, storks, fish eagles and terns, to eagles, lovebirds, parrots, cuckoos, bouboûs, woodpeckers, wagtails, chats, warblers, buntings and wydahs, found across the mixed woodlands, gorges and hills. Early mornings are sheer delight.

AGFA
PHOTO TIP
At full moon you can witness and capture the ghostly lunar rainbow over the Falls, particularly at **Devil's Cataract**. Lights from Zambia make it difficult to see the rainbow from that side. Ask at the Falls entrance as to the best times to see it.

WOOD CARVINGS
Try to avoid buying large sculptures carved from wood. The wood is often poached from hardwood forests, decimating beautiful indigenous trees in the process. Zimbabwe, the 'house of stone', has more than enough stone of any type to meet sculptors' and collectors' requirements.

Attractive curio displays line the road to the Victoria Falls.

THE RAIN FOREST

VERVET MONKEYS
The white and grey monkeys with powder-blue genitals that you see in the Rain Forest are vervets. Eyelid display and aggressive staring helps maintain the pecking order in troops of about 20. They have a repertoire of six alarm calls, such as one for leopard, another for eagle, and so on.

One of the best ways to view the Falls for the first time is by walking through the lush Rain Forest from Livingstone's Statue, which overlooks Devil's Cataract. The path winds in and out of the forest, affording different views of the Falls from various angles. The forest is rich in birds, wildlife, butterflies and plants.

The Rain Forest

Peace in the storm: in the rain forest you can hear the soft dripping of mist-drops off the leaves while the white thundering flood is only 60 m (200 ft) away. Rain forests have become one of the most powerful and evocative symbols of our threatened environment. The rain forest at the Victoria Falls, a UNESCO and World Heritage Site, weaves in and out of sun-sparkled viewpoints, eye-level with the churning white maelstrom. With its colourful butterflies and flowers, reedfrogs, spotted bushbuck, lush lianas and trees, it is the heritage of delicate, living beauty for all of us.

In the misty rain forest the air is heavy with birdsong and insects, the scent damp and rich. Take the narrow paved track past the Chain Walk, as it weaves through a dripping abundance of moss, strangler figs, swamp ferns, creepers, milkwoods and vines, root tangles, wild date palms, water berries, ironwood and zebrawood; it leads to viewpoints that face directly into the heart of the hurtling waterfall, a thunderous backdrop wherever you are in the forest.

Elephants sometimes break down the fences and wander into the rain forest, and warthogs push under the fences going in and out. Monkeys usually go where they please and occasionally lions leap over the fence. Paradise flycatchers, Heuglin's robins and black and white trumpeter hornbills are some of the birds found here, while spotted and

Restless Rain Forest resident: vervet monkey.

shy bushbuck and banded mongoose can be glimpsed by the observant.

Excluding the animals, over a million visitors per year come to the rain forest, but access is limited to 300 people at any one time. A small interpretive display is located at the thatched entrance just before the Victoria Falls Bridge opposite the parking lot.

Forest songster: Heuglin's robin.

PHOTO TIP

*Looking like bright red dandelions on mushroom stalks and making unusual subjects, **blood lilies** grow low and right to the edge of the **Rain Forest**. These pincushion blood lilies (Haemanthus multiflorus) are as big as cricket balls and flower from October to December.*

Wild date palms fringe the edge of the Rain Forest near Rainbow Falls.

THE TOWN

AGFA
PHOTO TIP
One-hour proccessing of colour photographs is easily available at the Falls. But a full range of photographic and video equipment is not widely available, so come equipped.

Victoria Falls is at times a sleepy village and at others, a hyper-active town running hundreds of thousands of visitors a year through the world's greatest outdoor theme park. The village lies between two national parks and on the edge of the town you may well meet lion, hippo, elephant or buffalo, especially at night.

Victoria Falls Town

The first settlement at the Victoria Falls was some 9 km (5.5 miles) upstream of today's town at the Old Drift in Zambia, where the wagons used to cross from Zimbabwe. Malaria deaths caused the settlers to move to higher ground, and with the coming of the railway bridge in 1905, Livingstone in Zambia became the main centre. The tourism of recent years, however, has favoured development on the Zimbabwean side.

INFORMATION BUREAU
On the corner of Parkway and Livingstone Way, the Information Bureau will tell all you need to know about the Falls, such as where to hire a bicycle, how to join a horse safari and when there will be a lunar rainbow over the Falls.

Victoria Falls is basically a two-road town: **Livingstone Way** is a continuation of the Bulawayo and airport road that runs past the Falls and over the bridge, while **Parkway** branches off Livingstone Way and runs past the attractive residential areas and hotels as far as the Zambezi National Park.

The urban area stretches across 3 km (2 miles), half of which is the village and leafy hilly suburbs, bounded by Courteney and Sopers Crescents, 1.5 km (1 mile) back from the Falls. The town is bisected by the railway which runs past the gracious Victoria Falls Hotel and visitors may watch old steam engines puffing and shunting across Livingstone Way, the town's main road, before the tracks turn to make the curve to the bridge into Zambia.

Banks, Air Zimbabwe, the Post Office, curios, The Falls Craft Village, and three large hotels are all east of the railway line, while practically everything else is on the other

Curios for Africa at the Victoria Falls 'Curio Row'.

THE TOWN **17**

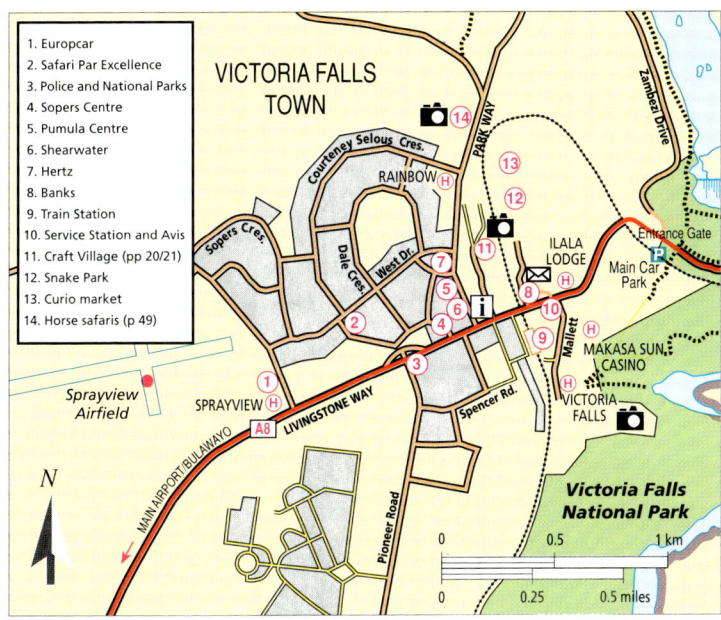

side of the track, including bicycles and scooters for hire, boutiques, restaurants, service stations, safari operators, and the town's inexpensive camp and chalet site. The town is a place for walking or cycling as nothing is further than 15 minutes away.

The **Sopers and Pumula Centres** are packed with white-water rafting, bungi-jumping and aircraft-flipping safari operators, all competing for your custom but refreshingly friendly and helpful too. Victoria Falls has managed to retain its village atmosphere in spite of big new hotels, direct flights to Cape Town and hundreds of thousands of visitors annually.

The best way to see the village is to go from the Victoria Falls Hotel to the Edwardian railway station, then to the Craft Village and 'curio row'. Backtracking to the railway crossing, go up Livingstone Way to the main town. A drive along Parkway and up the suburban roads will not only reveal lovely avenues of bougainvillaea and flowering tropical trees, but also a tiny aloe garden at Courteney Selous Corner.

> **SCOOT**
> Hire a 50 cc scooter from Scoot in the Pumula Centre and get a free first tank of fuel and unlimited Victoria Falls area mileage.

> **CAR HIRE**
> You can see much of the Falls on foot or bicycle, but at night you will need a car because of wild animals or if driving to the Zambezi National Park. **Europcar** is at the Sprayview Hotel, **Hertz** at Zimbank Building and **Avis** on Mellet Drive.

18 HANDY GUIDE VICTORIA FALLS

PHOTO TIP

*There are 140 species of tree and shrub fringing the Zambezi and in the Rain Forest, including a giant baobab along Zambezi Drive, 1.5 km (1 mile) from the Falls. Believed to be 1,000 years old, the **Big Tree** is 20 m (65 ft) round. Honey made from the white baobab flowers is delicious.*

Zambezi Drive

Zambezi Drive, which runs close to the Falls, features **the Big Tree**, a baobab believed to be 1,000 years old. Locals walk their dogs from here along the river to the A'Zambezi Hotel, a challenging stroll with crocs on the riverbank and lion in the bush.

Victoria Falls Hotel

The 1,000-year-old Big Tree.

The jewel in the crown, the oldest, most evocative, most carefully preserved hotel in the country, the Victoria Falls Hotel is a proper dowager empress, situated within earshot of the mighty Falls. Designed in 1904 before the First World War, it has generous, sweeping terraces, immaculate gardens and spacious rooms, a grand

Victoria Falls Hotel, cool, gracious elegance from the Africa of yesteryear.

hotel from the old world, rewired and renovated for the Internet age. The original railroad hotel was a structure of wood and corrugated iron built to accommodate the engineers working on the bridge. The dining room was a locomotive shed, while a retired train boiler provided steam for the laundry.

The hotel has survived visits from royalty, as well as one mortar shell attack from Zambia during the liberation war. The hotel's finances have survived a bookkeeper who went hunting and accidentally shot himself, and the hotel's illustrious reputation survived a maharajah who insisted on a ban on 'mixed swimming' because his serene dignity insisted that he swim unobserved by any ladies.

 RAILWAY STATION
Don't miss a visit to the Edwardian railway station with its puffing trains and mango trees. There's a daily evening run to Bulawayo at 18h00 arriving the following morning, and occasionally you'll see superbly equipped 'Istanbul Express' steam trains.

Take tea beneath the 200-year-old mahoganies on the patio, and stroll past the elegant columned veranda and admire the lily pond courtyard with its old trolley seat and cool bower of trees. Or sip a pink gin as the sunset over the Falls reflects its mist-pink glow.

The Hotel's doorman.

 **PHOTO TIP**
*The old-world **Victoria Falls Hotel** is colonial and orange-tiled, giving travellers an amazing view of the world's grandest waterfall and the high, criss-cross, steel arched bridge to Zambia. Guests are greeted by Oddwell, the long-serving badge-bedecked concierge.*

Chapel of St Mary Magdalene

Couples can get married in the Victoria Falls Hotel's small chapel of St Mary Magdalene, something that became popular with pilots who trained here during the Second World War and fell in love with local girls. It is still a popular practice for airline pilots today, the Falls being an idyllic and romantic honeymoon venue.

Inside the chapel, which was consecrated on 28 February 1932, are straight-backed, rather delicate chairs made of ilala palm weave. Phone the Victoria Falls Hotel on 4203 for further information.

Traditional dancing

Dance is everything in Africa: social, spiritual and instructional. Dance is prayer and ritual, an affirmation of authority and belonging. It is a giggling conversation between friends, a graduation ceremony from one stage of life to another. In Africa, dance is a way of life that is without any of the self-consciousness that sometimes inhibits other cultures.

 THE VICTORIA FALLS ADVERTISER:
Monday 3 October 1910, excerpt: 'Guests visiting the Victoria Falls Hotel, particularly the elderly, have commented that the walk to the Falls and back has proved somewhat exhausting. A hotel spokesman informed this reporter that plans were afoot to introduce rickshaws.'

CAMPING
The **Victoria Falls Town Camping Site** ('dome city') has good facilities and is right in the middle of the town between the railway line and the upper shopping centre with its entrance on Livingstone Way. There are camp sites further along the Zambezi River in the **National Park** – three with a hut – and you can camp at the game-viewing platform at **Chamabonda** if you book it in advance.

 PHOTO TIP
The traditional dancing in the evenings at the **Falls Craft Village** and **Victoria Falls Hotel** makes for spectacular photography where a flash is essential.

 TOUCH THE WILD
A three-hour tour conducted by Touch the Wild enables you to meet the local rural people of the Victoria Falls in their homes, tending their livestock, tilling their fields, building huts or teaching their children the traditional ways; tel. 4694.

Vibrant Makishi dancing, part of the traditional dance shows.

At the nightly **Traditional Dancing Show** at the **Falls Craft Village** you can see up to 75 dancers and drummers perform. A parable of Ngandu and Kanolo, the Crocodile and the Fisherman, is performed by a masked Tonga dancer in a multi-coloured bodysuit with two boys dancing inside a giant crocodile. The crocodile comes up behind the fisherman who is preoccupied with his fishing baskets, and four rhythmic drummers pound home the lesson of what happens to those who daydream on the river. There's also a Makishi dance 'thanking women for bringing up children', and another for welcoming circumcised boys back into the village after they've been away for three months in the bush being initiated into manhood.

Then, as the fires flicker on excited faces, young Shangaan men in an aggressive, whistling, clapping, foot-stomping dance fire up their spirits for battle, and prove to their elders that they can handle spears, shields and war. A victory dance, a funeral dance, high jumps, acrobatic air turns, painted men in acrobatic stilt dances, spirits possessed by ancestors, dancers with fantastic masks bigger than they are, and *Nzingi Mutwe*, a masked dance for the chief's Head Councillor and Beer Taster, are all performed here.

The Craft Village, tel. 4309, is just behind the Post Office. The other traditional dance option, **Africa Spectacular**, takes place each night at 19h00 at the **Victoria Falls Hotel**, where vibrant Makishi folk dancing is performed outdoors in a specially constructed *kraal*; tel. 4203 for more information.

 The Falls Craft Village
A walking lecture tour through the colourful Falls Craft Village shows thatched huts, chicken coops, iron smelting furnaces, and kitchens of six

 CURIOS AND CRAFTS

*The road past the Falls Craft Village behind the post office has been nicknamed '**Curio Row**'. There are also shops here, including **Sopers** (established 1911) and **Jairos Jiri** which sells good Binga baskets, originally made in Binga but now also at Victoria Falls. There is plenty of stone sculpture and crochet-work at the far end. Look out for the small hunter-gatherer figures.*

Sculptor at work bringing life out of wood.

Traditional n'anga *divining the future for you.*

> ### DAISY, DAISY ...
> A great way to explore the town and Falls area, and quite the local custom, is to hire a bicycle. Try **Bushtrackers** in Parkway for starters. There are several other companies offering this service but some bikes are a touch rickety.

> ### PHOTO TIP
> Make sure you have an adaptor to charge and run your video batteries from 12v DC vehicle batteries and 220v AC power source, and a long lead. If staying in a hotel, you should be able to charge the batteries there.

different Zimbabwean ethnic groups. On display are the common items of traditional life: spears, baskets, drums, fish traps, beer filters and ostrich eggs with a hole in the top, used by San 'Bushmen' for carrying water.

A Tonga childrens' sleeping hut is set on stilts to protect the children from lions and other predators, the ladder removed at night. There are grain bins with entrances so small that only a child can climb in to hand over the stored grains inside.

Living huts vary from a small, dome-shaped, twig-and-thatch shelter of the wandering, nomadic San people to the large pole-and-mudplaster Venda Chief's hut with painted, decorated walls, crocodile motifs and an interior 'guard corridor'.

Also displayed is a Shona *dare*, or men's meeting place, where women are not allowed, a Shona hut where the bodies of important leaders would be smoked dry before burial, and a resident *n'anga*, or spirit medium and traditional healer, who coughs to announce his presence and who, for a small fee, will throw a set of carved bones and tell your future.

The tour ends, conveniently, in a large curio shop with practically every fast-sell item on sale in Africa; tel. 4309 for more details.

WINING AND DINING

At least 25 restaurants are found at the Victoria Falls, many in the large hotels. All of the non-hotel restaurants are in the Sopers-Pumula complex at the corner of Parkway and Livingstone Way. Fast foods, such as **Naran's Indian Takeaways** and **Eatapizza** (open from 10h00 to midnight) are also available.

Village grub

Ever-popular is the cornerhouse **Wimpy** in Parkway serving fast food burgers and chips. Five minutes away in the Pumula Centre, the **Cattleman** serves

THE TOWN

Ilala Lodge: elegant patio dining overlooking lawns and bush.

American-style steaks. The **Pizza Bistro** is intimate, family-run and serves handsome-sized pizzas. The music and laughter next door come from the popular **Explorer's Pub**, hub of rafters, safari guides, hearty pub grub and a thousand tall stories.

Hotel fare

The **Ilala Hotel Restaurant**, seating 120, is the last building on the left going towards the bridge. It is a good, professional eatery with outside patio dining. For romantics, visit the **Makasa Sun Casino Hotel** where you can eat by lamplight in the open-air dining area round the pool. En route to the Zambezi National Park is the perfectly sited pool patio of the **A'Zambezi Hotel** on the banks of the Zambezi River. Poolside restaurants also feature at the **Sprayview** and **Rainbow Hotels**, both in lovely settings. Some 4 km (2.5 miles) from the village near the Victoria Falls Safari Lodge is the popular **Boma Restaurant**, their speciality being *potjiekos* (a many

> **DRINKING WATER**
> Water from hotel taps at Victoria Falls has been treated. It's safe to drink but you can often taste the chemicals. Bottled water is for sale in supermarkets and bottle stores.

The A'Zambezi Hotel is superbly situated on the banks of the river.

SADZA
Delicious when freshly cooked, this stiff maize (corn) flour porridge is the country's national dish. Sadza is usually eaten with a relish of rape (spinach), peanut butter or stewed beef or goat, using fingers only.

PHOTO TIP

If you want to take a photograph of the local people, it is polite to always ask first and perhaps offer a prearranged tip.

layered stew cooked in a three-legged cast-iron pot). The Victoria Falls Safari Lodge boasts the **Makuwakuwa Restaurant** set beneath soaring Balinese thatch with views over a water hole and the African bush. The **Elephant Hills Hotel** has several restaurants, one of which overlooks a long, twisting curve of the Zambezi.

By far the most elegant place to dine is the **Livingstone Room** at the Victoria Falls Hotel where, in the claret and cream high-ceilinged dining saloon, discreet waiters serve *haute-cuisine* and you can listen to the *Debvu* (old beards) playing reprises of yesteryear. The hotel also has two other restaurants, including a patio barbecue with marimba band.

Dining in Zambia
Best by the Falls, especially for weekend buffets, is the **Mosi-oa-Tunya Inter-Continental Hotel**, tel (260) 3-321210, while nearby the **Rainbow Lodge**, tel (269) 3-322473, has the best river view.

GAMBLING

Zimbabwe is quite coy about casinos. It allows them to be run only in holiday resort areas, such as the Victoria Falls where there are two: at the Makasa Sun and the Elephant Hills Hotel (see p 27). Visitors play and are paid in forex and the atmosphere is holiday rather than serious money-making. The casinos have blacklists which not only cover undesirables but also whizz kids who have mastered such casino-milking systems as labouchère.

Makasa Sun
Ian Smith opened the Makasa Sun Casino nine days after the Unilateral Declaration of Independence on 20 November 1965. It has recently been refurbished in what management describes as the 'Raffles look'. Some of the aristrocratic machines, which were found in the cellars and restored, date back to the very earliest days.

Eighty per cent of customers are tourists, with bets on the slot machines winning up to $20,000 – the house keeps 10%. Contact the Makasa Sun Casino on 4275 or the Elephant Hills Hotel on tel. 4793 for further details.

GAMBLING
The four main games played in Zimbabwe casinos are blackjack, banco, Zambezi (stud) poker and American roulette.

PHOTO TIP
*At the **Elephant Camp** close to the Falls, visitors, seated in howdahs and led by an armed guide, are taken on four young elephants into the wild. These game safaris, seen from the great height of the elephant, are something special; tel. 2004, fax 4349, P O Box 159, Victoria Falls.*

Mahoot guides take guests on elephant back safaris near the Zambezi National Park.

AROUND AND ABOUT VICTORIA FALLS

LANGUAGE
Shona, with its six main dialects, is the mother tongue to 67% of the population of Zimbabwe, while **Ndebele** is spoken by 15%. The Victoria Falls people are traditionally **Tonga**. All the street signs and nearly every newspaper in Zimbabwe is in **English**; it is the language of television news, policemen and taxi drivers.

ELEPHANT TUSK GRAVEYARDS
The Leya, Subiya and Toka used to show reverence to their dead by surrounding graveyards with elephant tusks stuck into the earth.

Leaving the town, drive 6 km (4 miles) along Parkway to reach the Zambezi National Park, great for fishing and game-viewing trips. En route you'll pass the turn-off to the Elephant Hills Hotel, and further along is the Crocodile Ranch, just 5 km (3 miles) from town.

THE ELEPHANT HILLS HOTEL
The huge, Aztec-type Elephant Hills Hotel, with its casino and world-famous golf course, lies sprawled on a hill overlooking the golf course and the spray of the Falls. Contact the Hotel on 13-4793 for more information.

Golf course
Warthogs love this golf course on the banks of the Zambezi River, the Bermuda grass and rolling fairways with tender roots providing gourmet fare for them. They love it so much, that daily they charge the fence between the Zambezi National Park and the golf course.

Impala, kudu, waterbuck and lion sometimes leap over the fence, and a section of 4-cm-thick steel cables (1½-in) sunk in concrete has been put in to keep the hippos out – the Zambezi River is only 500 m (⅓ mile) away. When you've got the longest, most enchanting

The Elephant Hills Hotel overlooks its 18-hole golf course and the spray of the Falls.

championship golf course in southern Africa, word gets around. An old rule here was that you got a free drop if your ball landed in a warthog dig, but now you have to play it as it lies. If lion appear on the course, you are advised not to play at all.

A golfing magazine once stated succinctly: 'Novel hazards and sights. Don't ignore the warning sign about the crocodiles in the reed-fringed water hazards.'

The ever-questing warthog.

Birding trails

This is one of those golf courses that can genuinely claim to be much more than a golf course. You can explore its length by following laid-out nature trails and the hotel has a checklist to help you identify trumpeter hornbills, red bishops, cormorants, darters and many other birds. Stop at a bench under a shade tree to watch the animals and golfers in natural mopane woodland where baobabs, ilala palms and several species of acacia trees thrive.

Casino

Besides boasting a championship 18-hole golf course, regular gambling tournaments are also held here. The casino is more costly than the Makasa Sun (*see* p 25) with minimum bets at $25 and $50, and you won't be allowed in if you are wearing jeans.

THE ZAMBEZI NATURE SANCTUARY

At the Zambezi Nature Sanctuary, 5 km (3 miles) upstream of the Falls, is the crocodile ranch, a leather shop, a wildcat orphanage with caracals and leopards, the old 'Crocarosity' shop, shady riverbank tea room, children's farmyard, and an open 'vulture restaurant' where these street fighters of the African bush come to squabble over leftovers.

Crocodile ranch

Ten thousand crocodiles, graded by age and size, bask in long pools beneath shady trees, while a breeding group lies open mouthed in the sun beside the sanctuary's stream and reed beds, whitecrowned plovers pecking for parasites among their teeth. Watch a 'Big Daddy' croc go for a hunk of raw meat at feeding time. There's

PHOTO TIP

*Crocodiles have remained unchanged for 140 million years. Capture these prehistoric creatures on film at the **Zambezi Nature Sanctuary**. Ninety eight per cent of baby crocodiles die in infancy, often from pneumonia. All crocodiles swallow stones to help their digestion, and, contrary to popular belief, they prefer fresh to decomposed meat. Fish, however, is their staple diet.*

MALARIA

Never underestimate this ancient disease. Transmitted by the Anopheles mosquito (as opposed to the Culex pipiens, or common mosquito), the disease was known to the Romans. The word comes from Italian, mal'aria (bad air) as it was believed that the air of swampy districts carried it. Take medication before, during and after your stay.

Cold-blooded crocodiles bask in the morning sun.

🍴 CROCODILE TAILS
A tiny section of the tails of crocodiles are made into a variety of entrées at the Falls restaurants; some are smoked and served with mayonnaise or lemon. They taste rather like crayfish. Crocodile ranches are big-business in Zimbabwe, with large waterside compounds at the Victoria Falls, Kariba and many other sites throughout the country.

🍴 PICNICS
*You may enjoy eating your sandwiches on a rustic bench in the Rain Forest overlooking the Falls, or by the road on the way to the airport. But the best spots are along the river and Chamabonda Drive in the **Zambezi National Park**. Be aware of wild animals, including crocodiles.*

a sudden sideways jerk of his head, then a snap of long snaggletooth jaws, followed by ripping and tearing. They'll let you hold a baby crocodile in your hand at this ranch, but remember someday he'll become a 500-kg hunter-killer (1,100 pounds) that can leap 7 m (23 ft) and for those crucial moments, run faster than you can.

A fixed proportion of crocodiles are returned to the wild yearly by the sanctuary as these creatures are vital to a balanced river and fish ecology. Crocodiles eat large barbel catfish which decimate the smaller fish. If these small fish are wiped out, 40 species of fishing birds would not survive. The 15 crocodile farms in the country also produce leather goods and meat, and have ensured the survival of this ancient species in Zimbabwe.

The Crocodile Ranch can be found along Parkway and is open from 08h00-17h00; tel. 4637.

ZAMBEZI NATIONAL PARK
The lovely wooded Zambezi National Park of 57,000 ha (140,847 acres) stretches 38 km (24 miles) to the Matetsi Safari Area in the west and south from the river for 24 km (15 miles). It is flanked by a strip of big tree riverine forest that includes such giants as *Acacia albida* whose pods elephant love, multi-limbed fig trees, ebonies, mangosteens, ilala palms and giant baobabs.

🏠 Fishing and camping sites
At the park and on the river are 25 fishing and camping sites, often named after small tributaries, such as **Mpala Jena** and **Siamunungu**, overlooking rapids where elephant and other game cross the river.

The National Parks have their lodges in the Zambezi National Park, only 6 km (4 miles) from the Falls. Each lodge is separated by bush and graceful ilala palms, and they are regularly visited by ever-questing warthogs. The entrance to the park is decorated with the twin skulls of kudu horns locked to the death.

AROUND AND ABOUT VICTORIA FALLS

The river is often 2 km (1.5 miles) wide in the park and a circular gravel road, a continuation of Parkway, winds past the site for float plane safaris, then along this riverine section for 50 km (30 miles), dropping down to the river at half a dozen secluded spots. The National Parks office in Livingstone Way will provide you with accommodation details; tel. 4558.

Wildlife

You will find practically every type of game in the park, which has particularly fine herds of the scimitar-horned sable antelope; these animals have been known to challenge and even kill lion. Elephant, hyaena, zebra, waterbuck, leopard, cheetah, the mottled wild dog and, always, the high-jumping impala, are well represented. Because of its mixed habitats, the park also offers excellent birding. Crocodiles, which you will see basking along the river, were once nearly extinct as a result of indiscriminate hunting, but now that the river has been restocked by a commercial crocodile farm, they are as evident as ever.

Cheetahs, fastest of all animals.

Game lodges and pans

West of the park, the Kazungula Road leads to the **Matetsi Private Game Reserve** with 18 km (11 miles) of river frontage (tel. [27] 11-8038421), with **Imbabala** (tel. 2004/4219) and **Westwood Game Lodge** (tel. 4614) nearby. Six kilometres (4 miles) south of Victoria Falls and close to the Zambezi National Park is Chamabonda Gate; the **Masuwe Lodge** (tel. 426512) is 3 km (2 miles) further. The road from Chamabonda Gate will take you to **Kaliankuo Pan** with its hide, and **Njako Pan**, also with its game-viewing platform. Sleep at **Chamabonda platform** to hear the eerie whoop of hyaena.

AGFA PHOTO TIP

An instamatic is fine for campfire snaps but not really any good for wildlife shots. You'll be able, because of the brightness, to work with 50 or 100 ISO/ASA ratings. 400 is good for the early mornings or evenings.

DEATH OF LIVINGSTONE

Livingstone inspired a generation. He did much to end the ravages of the slave trade and was persistent in his almost mystical pursuit of the source of the Nile. Found dead, kneeling in prayer by the side of his camp cot, two of his African colleagues cut out and buried his heart, then carried his body to the coast to be buried later in Westminster Abbey.

NATIONAL PARKS CHALETS

Normally booked at Harare's Central Reservations Office, the chalets, 6 km (4 miles) down Parkway, give each holiday family a wide slice of the Zambezi riverbank from which to admire ilala palms, cruise boats and warthogs.

THE RIVER

SOPERS
Jack Soper was the tollkeeper of the Victoria Falls Bridge when it opened in 1905. Crocodile hunter, photographer and colourful character, his reputation, like those of other river 'drifters', was extraordinary. He once hung by a rope around his ankles to get a photo of the chasm. The curio shop he started is still open in the Falls village.

ZAMBEZI RIVER
The Zambezi is the fourth largest river in Africa after the Nile, Zaire and Niger. It is 2,704 km (1,680 miles) long and rises in Zambia, flows through Angola, fringes the Caprivi, leaps over the Falls and forms Lake Kariba. It then flows past Mana Pools, forms the Cahora Bassa lake in Mozambique and enters the Indian Ocean 200 km (125 miles) north of Beira port.

The Zambezi is born as a small spring 1,000 km (621 miles) from the Falls in the northwestern uplands of Zambia. In the beginning the flow is barely strong enough to float a flower on, but gradually as it drifts past acacia and fig groves, papyrus swamps and flood plains, its strength builds. Upstream of the Falls the Zambezi can host a calm, leisurely cruise, while downstream it churns into swirling rapids, ideal for white-water rafting and kayaking.

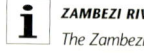 The Victoria Falls Bridge

This bridge is the quintessential image of an age gone by, symbolic of the power, skill and financial muscle of the Victorian empire builders. Many opposed the bridge being built, such as Rhodes' own brother Frank (who prayed for an earthquake to halt construction), and still today there are those who want to improve the view by taking it down and replacing it with a modern structure upriver.

The bridge is an expansion-jointed, tar-over-steel highway for cars, trucks, trains and pedestrians. It was built in 1905 as part of Rhodes' Cape to Cairo railway. The highest of its kind at the time, the bridge is 111 m (364 ft) above the water. The superstructure contains 1,540 tonnes of steel, and is 198 m (650 ft) long. The main arch is 152 m (499 ft) in length.

The whole bridge was prefabricated in England, assembled, taken to pieces, then transported to the Falls by ship and train. At 7am on 1 April 1905, before the sun got too hot and the steel expanded, the centre piece was lowered into position and

bolted. It was widened and reinforced in 1930 to allow for road traffic, and further reinforced in 1980. The old come just to marvel at it, the dedicated to take videos and the adventurous for the world's highest, most spectacular bungi-jump.

It's a great people-watching spot: Zambian women with pushcarts full of second-hand clothing to sell in Zimbabwe; Zambian kids selling frozen, coloured, flavoured water out of buckets of ice; Indian women in colourful saris; and young people wearing the overland-truck-tour uniform of denim shorts, trade bead necklaces, ankle chains, rafter sandals and tie-dyed T-shirts.

PHOTO TIP

*The **Victoria Falls Bridge** looks in silhouette like a Victorian laced-steel half-moon. It is visible from the Victoria Falls Hotel, and on the Zambian side from the rocks below Palm Grove. This is a good place to photograph the death-defying bungi-jumpers.*

FISHING

*The Zambezi provides good fishing and many a shady spot, such as **Sansinba**, **Mpala Jena** and **Kandahar**, overlooking rapids and game. Some 84 species of fish occur, ranging from tigerfish to greenhead bream, large catfish, vundu, labeo and above all, the fighting African pike. Boats can be hired at the Falls.*

The Victoria Falls Bridge, built in 1905 as part of Cecil John Rhodes' Cape to Cairo railway, spans the narrowest point of the gorge below the Falls.

Intrepid kayakers are dwarfed by the immense cliffs of the Victoria Falls.

THE RIVER

The first bungi-jump

In 1878 Major A. de Serpa Pinto measured the Falls with a sextant by leaning over the edge, supported by a cloth tied around his waist and held by two porters. But it was Jack Soper, the colourful originator of Soper's Curios and tollkeeper of the Victoria Falls bridge, who can claim to be the first bungi-jumper in 1905. He had himself lowered 31 m (100 ft) down into the chasm opposite the Falls so that he could capture a particularly unusual photo angle.

Bungi-jumping today

Step up. Don't look down. And then jump off the 111 m-high (364 ft) Victoria Falls Bridge with a rubber band tied around your ankles. For the first 40 m (130 ft) you're in free fall, flying like a skydiver. Then the bungi begins to stretch and you decelerate some 60 m (200 ft), much more gently than you imagined. Then an amazing reversal of forces occurs, and up you go, 80% of the way back to the bridge where you started and you hang weightless above the Zambezi's rock-tumbling fury below. Then comes this strange feeling of elation – you survived!

The world's highest, most beautiful bungi-jump.

Today the aptly named African Extreme, started by New Zealanders, operates the world's highest and undoubtedly most beautiful bungi-jump in the world. Book at the Bridge, at Shearwater (tel. 4471), Valley Ventures in Zambia (tel. (260) 3-320742) or through an agent. It's not cheap, don't do it if you have a knee injury, and it's certainly a sport for the adventurous.

Batoka Gorge

The Batoka Gorge is the Zambezi River's Grand Canyon: a maze of switchback, zigzag canyons cut like rapier slashes through volcanic rock from the dinosaur age. This is an epic, lost-in-time world, eagle country where raptors nest in high lookouts and soar on rising air

TAITA FALCON
The rare falcon, named after the Teita (sic) area of Kenya, can be seen in the July-October breeding season in the cliffs and gorges of the Zambezi below the Falls. Solitary or in pairs, this strong flier (*Falco fasciinucha*) that pounces on bats and swifts, has a short tail and un-flecked browny-white underparts; 433 species of bird are found within 100 km (62 miles) of Victoria Falls.

PHOTO TIP
If you want to video the **bungi-jumping**, it is best not to use automatic focus. The moments leading up to the jump are usually the most spell-binding when fear, courage and resolution play over the jumper's face.

FISH EAGLE
First recorded in southern Africa in 1800 at the Keurbooms River in the Cape, the fish eagle's echoing 'kow, kow' is one of the unforgettable sounds of Africa and of the whole Zambezi riverine system, stretching back to the Caprivi and east to Kariba and Mana Pools.

Meal near the maelstrom; rafters stop for lunch in the Batoka Gorge.

thermals while looking for rock dassies to snatch. If you're very lucky, you might see the rare creamy-brown taita falcon diving silently on any bird or bat that looks like a good meal.

On a white-water rafting expedition, you can (in-between the roller-coaster cavalry charges) float quietly through the Batoka Gorge. Figs and fever trees, ebonies, even a few baobabs, struggle desperately for a living among the rocks. In the dry season the gorge has a desert feeling to it, and in the rainy season the grasses and trees come to life and splash the canyon walls with new green growth. When it rains, flash waterfalls come spilling down from the 200-m-high canyon rims (660 ft) above the gorge, and the spray blows into the rain and over your head – it's pure magic!

If you're not doing the raft trip, the quickest and easiest way to get into the gorge is the steep, root-scramble descent directly in front of the Victoria Falls Hotel.

Lagoons, lakes and caves

There are two limestone caves in the Batoka Gorge; several near Rapid No. 9 have been explored, revealing an Aladdin's wonderland of stalagmites and stalagtites. Part way along the 100-km (62-mile) Gorge,

PHOTO TIP

*There is not much point in taking a camera when **white-water rafting**. You will need both hands to hang onto the raft and you don't need the added worry of possibly losing a camera (which would need to be a sub-aqua model). The best shots are taken from the riverbanks or above the gorge, and there are professional photographers on the banks who do the necessary. Photographs and videos of your rafting trip are displayed and sold the same night at Ilala Lodge.*

the river opens out into a lagoon, a popular fishing area. Here the Msuna River joins the Zambezi before closing in again for 30 km (20 miles), leading eventually to **Devil's Gorge**, **Mlibizi** and the headwaters of **Lake Kariba**.

White-water rafting

White-water rafting on the mighty Zambezi is sheer excitement, sheer terror, sheer exhilaration. This is Mother Nature's original river roller-coaster ride through the Batoka Gorge below the Falls. Often called the 'wildest one-day white-water rafting run in the world', you'll zigzag through a maze of sheer-drop canyons, being bucked and tumbled through 19 rapids with 200 m (660 ft) cliffs on either side and, at times, 100 m (330 ft) of dark, twisting water beneath you. The Avon inflatable raft plunges through rapids with names such as Jaws of Death, Oblivion, Devil's Toilet Bowl and Rapid 13, 'the mother'. You'll bounce and twist, buckle and slide, as waves bury you in swirling, foaming white water.

Steered by an oarsman shouting commands to the scrum line in the bow to shift weight, you punch 'n roll through giant stopper waves and hang on with a 'white knuckle death grip' – do it right and you'll emerge cheering and laughing. Helmets and life vests are provided, also wet-suit tops in winter. Safety kayakers paddle alongside to quickly pick up anyone who falls overboard. In an emergency, a helicopter can be called in by radio. A very steep climb into and out of the gorge means that you must be reasonably fit, and at least 16 years of age.

ZAMBEZI FEET

Rafters, a black rubber sandal with fancy coloured straps, is the Victoria Falls shoe. Cool, convenient and comfortable, wear it in or out of the water (when rafting). The other local favourite is the 'vellie', a suede desert boot worn without socks by men of the bush. The Courteney Boot is for serious hikers.

ZAMBEZI RIVER FESTIVAL

One of the first regattas on the river was held in 1905 and included a royal Lozi barge race. 1995 heralded the Camel International White-Water Challenge. In October each year there are river races, and white-water rafting competitions down the Batoka Gorge. It attracts top teams from all over the world and is screened to 30 million TV audiences worldwide.

CRUEL DIVINITY

Missionary **François Coillard** wrote in 1878 '... local people believe that the Falls are haunted by a malevolent and cruel divinity, and they make it offerings, a bead necklace, a bracelet, which they fling into the abyss.'

'The wildest one-day white-water rafting run in the world.'

PHOTO TIP

*Stately, tall, northern **ilala palms** line the Zambezi above the Falls in lovely sunset silhouette. The best way to capture these on film is by taking a sunset cruise on the river. The palms grow in a long riverine swathe from the Zambezi west to the Caprivi, Okavango and Cunene rivers. Salt 'n pepper sets are made from the vegetable ivory and the wine from the sap is almost as good as coconut tree toddy.*

Rafting operators

Sobek, the American Company, were the first to run the Zambezi; they have pioneered many rivers worldwide. Next came a group of Harare schoolboys on a bamboo raft and inflated tyres. Safari Par Excellence is the only company that offers trips from both sides of the river, while Shearwater, the largest rafting and canoeing operator, and Frontiers, begin their trips on the Zimbabwean side, directly below the Victoria Falls Hotel. Half-day or full day trips are the norm but a recommended special is overnight camping in the spectacular Batoka Gorge. Check the Advisory on page 63 for the various white-water rafting operators.

Rafting fever

Rafting has become the great experience at Victoria Falls and each year 40 000 people take the wild river one-day expedition which normally operates from July through to mid-March. At Victoria Falls they have a saying: ride the river once and you'll be back – it's like a fever in the blood. The Batoka Gorge may soon be flooded by an ecologically catastrophic dam, ending all white-water rafting.

CRUISING ABOVE THE FALLS

Canoeing and kayaking

Paddling easily and gliding silently with the river, you soon relax and begin to feel the magic: bee-eaters dressed like 60s rock stars in outrageous blues and purples and greens as they swoop to catch insects in the air, or a giant kingfisher gazing at you from a sausage tree branch.

You pass sandbars with basking crocodiles who slither underwater to get away; explore narrow channels overgrown with trees and land on

Canoeing, a peaceful way to explore the Zambezi.

Sociable sundowner cruises begin above the Falls.

uninhabited islands, then paddle quickly away from a sudden submarine upthrust of an angry, snorting hippopotamus. Hippos displaying side-tooth yawning are aggressive guardians of their water territories.

There are wild, but fun, grade two rapids to run, impala, kudu, waterbuck, and elephant who shake the ilala palms to knock the vegetable ivory fruit down. And if you're really lucky, you might see one swimming in the river with a rolling underwater running motion, trunk held high above the water like a periscope.

Every kind of canoe and kayak safari is available above the Falls, from a day or half-day trip, to a four-day trip starting at Kazungula in the west with overnight stops at various safari camps. For canoeing and kayaking trips, contact Shearwater (tel. 4471).

River cruises

There are 20 different cruise boats above the Falls offering breakfast cruises (with sparkling wine to toast the dawn, or continental breakfast or a full eggs and bacon feast), tea at Kanahar island cruises, booze cruises, sundowner cruises, and best of all, the gentle bank-hugging 'wine route' canoe cruises.

Consult the Visitor's Digest on page 63 for details on the various river options.

BUFFALO
The mud-wallowing buffalo, with its massive body and curved horns, weighs close to 800 kg (1 764lb). There are 50,000 buffalo in Zimbabwe, a handful of whom have been domesticated for draught power. The animal is plentiful on the shores of the Zambezi, and game-viewing from a boat allows close encounters. Buffalo are known to be highly dangerous to marauding humans; it is said the mark of a crack hunter is to face a charging buffalo in the open with two rounds, then walk away.

PEACE FALLS
*'Victoria Falls, peerless jewel of Africa! Soul-stirring power, Breath-taking beauty, Life-elevating majesty!' On 2 January 1996 the **Victoria Falls** was declared a **Sri Chinmoy Peace Falls**. It joins a family of over 800 significant landmarks around the world that have been dedicated to peace. Sri Chinmoy is an ambassador of peace and has dedicated his life to fostering it.*

EXCURSIONS

AGFA
PHOTO TIP
If you are taking aerial shots, a high shutter speed of say 1/500 seconds will compensate for the vibration of the aircraft. A 50mm lens is recommended.

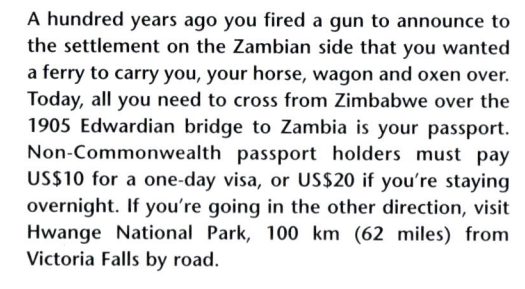

A hundred years ago you fired a gun to announce to the settlement on the Zambian side that you wanted a ferry to carry you, your horse, wagon and oxen over. Today, all you need to cross from Zimbabwe over the 1905 Edwardian bridge to Zambia is your passport. Non-Commonwealth passport holders must pay US$10 for a one-day visa, or US$20 if you're staying overnight. If you're going in the other direction, visit Hwange National Park, 100 km (62 miles) from Victoria Falls by road.

Flight of the Angels

Terry Spencer (founder of today's Crocodile Ranch) was the first man to fly an airplane under the Victoria Falls Bridge, and then he spent the rest of his life denying that he'd done it, for fear of losing his pilot's licence. It was also Terry who began the tradition of the Flight of Angels over the Falls. In the beginning, it was a one-man show and if Terry didn't feel like it, there was no flight that day. Since then, consumer choice has come to town, and for your sky safari you have a smorgasbord of options, including a microlight flight, the modern version of the open cockpit, goggles-and-white-scarf flying of 80 years ago.

RAIL SAFARIS
*Twice a month old-fashioned steam trains, operated by **Rail Safaris of Bulawayo**, head north from Bulawayo through Hwange National Park to Victoria Falls, offering old-style elegance and stylish game-viewing.*

A helicopter safari gives visitors an unusual view of the Zambezi.

Sky safaris

The most nostalgic flight of all is in a pontoon, converted Cessna 185 seaplane that skims the river in a long, slightly rocking take-off between islands. In 1948 BOAC launched a flying boat service from England to the Victoria Falls but this was withdrawn in 1950. Today, the booze cruise boats line up to watch the float plane take-offs. The pontoons are divided into rather small, individual compartments, rather like a submarine, and are continually checked for leaks caused by the flexing of the metal.

Fixed-wing aircraft and helicopter flights are offered in a bewildering variety of Dawn Patrols, Dusk Patrols, Sky Safaris, Angel Flights and Falls Skyviews over the rafting gorges and game parks, and even a helicopter flight that lands on a Zambezi River island for a champagne breakfast. There have been complaints about the unrestricted and continuous flights of the helicopters whose intrusive air-thumping overhead at the Falls can be as noisy as a Vietnam war movie.

Float plane tours are reminiscent of the flying boats of yesteryear.

For more information on these flights, contact the Victoria Falls Publicity Association, corner Parkway and Livingstone Way, tel. 4202.

THE EASTERN BANK

Crossing into Zambia is only a short walk over the Victoria Falls Bridge. Immediately to the left of customs lies **Palm Grove**, **Knife Edge**, **Eastern Cataract**, a **curio market** and a small early man **Field Museum**. The museum, a worthwhile visit, is open daily from 10h30-17h00 and an entrance fee is charged.

The **Musi-oa-Tunya Intercontinental Hotel** is the closest hotel to the Falls – tel. (260) 3-321210 – followed by **Rainbow Lodge**, 1 km (just over half a mile) from the border, tel. (260) 3-321806. A dreadlocked band in leopard skin outfits plays Lobale Singubu music facing a lovely wide sweep of the river above the Falls. The hotel, with its of view of hippos, elephants, the rising mist clouds and rainbows of the Falls and Livingstone Island, is one that every hotel investor group in the world is trying to get from the Zambian government.

CAPE TOWN DIRECT
Every Saturday, Air Zimbabwe flies direct to Cape Town and back from Victoria Falls, linking two of Africa's top attractions. The other two are Egypt's pyramids and East Africa's Serengeti.

KAZANGULA
Kazangula, 70 km (45 miles) west of the Falls and the truck-ferry crossing point on the Zambezi where Zimbabwe, Zambia and Botswana meet (with Namibia's Caprivi 55 km; 35 miles away), is a dusty petrol stop of open plains. Safari lodges nearby include Imbabala, Westwood and Matetsi Game Reserve.

Calm at the end of the day: the islands and gorges bathed in the sun's last rays.

Livingstone Island

Missionary, explorer and liberator, David Livingstone was the hero of his age. It was from **Kalai Island** upriver of the Falls that Livingstone set forth on the morning of 16 November 1855 in a Kololo canoe. It was his journey above the Falls, gliding past lush islands with flowering trees, graceful palms, white-plumed reeds, hippos, baobabs, gentle rapids and meandering channels, that Livingstone described thus 'Scenes so lovely must have been gazed on by angels in their flight'. Writers ever since have appropriated his words to describe the Falls.

Livingstone finally reached the island on the edge of the Falls that was to be named after him, and 'no one could perceive where the vast body of water went, it seemed to lose itself in the earth'. He crept forward in awe and peered over the edge to see 'the most wonderful sight I had witnessed in Africa...dense white cloud...two bright rainbows...myriads of small currents rushing in one direction'.

He named the awesome wonder the Victoria Falls, carved his name on what was probably a *muchenje*, or African ebony tree (*Diospyros mespiliformis*), which has long since disappeared, and planted peach and apricot trees, coffee and nuts on this, his 'garden island'. In 1860 Livingstone returned to the area and, among other things, made a careful measurement of the Falls.

There is a tented camp hidden in the trees on the island, run by the Zambian-based Tongabezi (tel. [260] 3-323235), who offer a waiter-served lunch a few feet from the edge of the abyss. Zambian canoe safari operators, such as Makora Quest (tel. [260] 3-321679), will paddle you along Dr Livingstone's route to where he spent the night camped on Kalai Island, and to Livingstone Island where he crawled to the edge.

Contact the National Tourist Board in Zambia for further information on tel. (260) 3-321404.

HUNTING SAFARIS

Vast tracks of land near the Falls have been set aside as **Hunting Safari Areas**. Zimbabwe believes that the only way to save its game is to give it a value (hunters pay very high fees) and to share the rewards with local communities as part of the **Campfire Project**.

AGFA PHOTO TIP

Hippo is Greek for 'water horse'. The many flotillas of hippo which you see in the Zambezi are known as pods or rafts. A hippo can submerge and walk along the river bottom for 7 minutes, but still hear, see and smell as if it were on the surface. Hippo can outrun a man and easily destroy a boat. Watch out for their wide-mouthed warning yawns.

Pods, or rafts, of hippo are a common sight in the Zambezi.

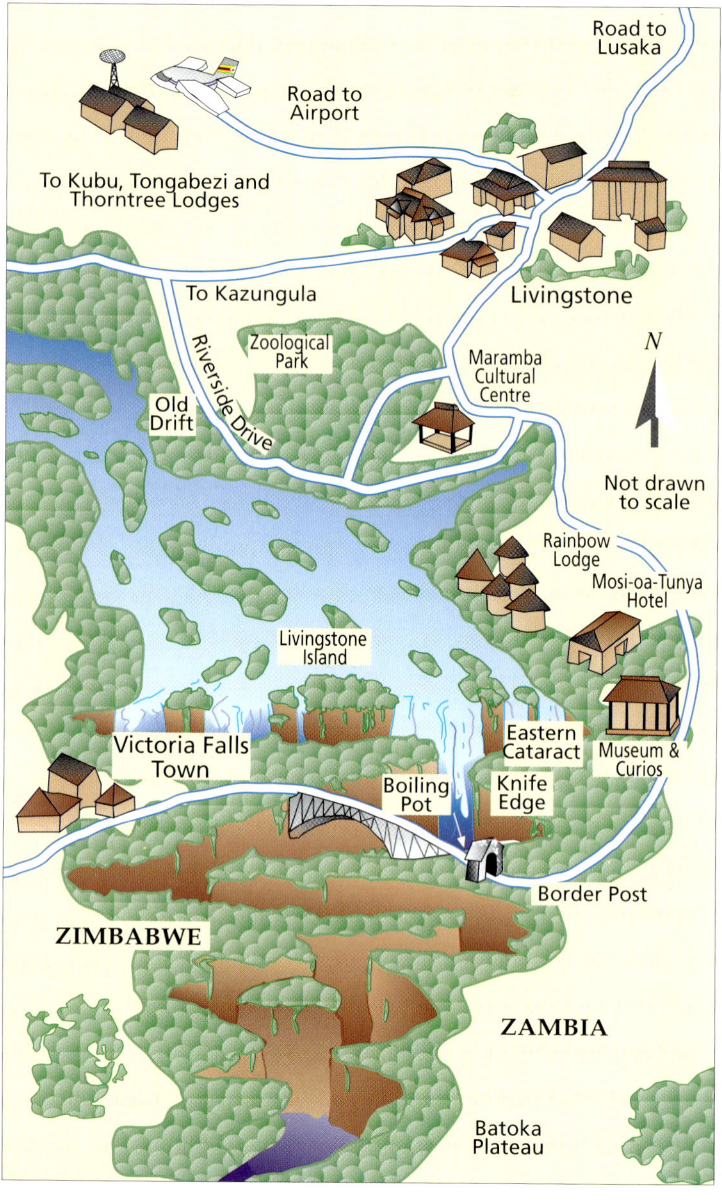
Road to Lusaka
Road to Airport
To Kubu, Tongabezi and Thorntree Lodges
To Kazungula
Livingstone
Riverside Drive
Zoological Park
Maramba Cultural Centre
N
Old Drift
Not drawn to scale
Rainbow Lodge
Mosi-oa-Tunya Hotel
Livingstone Island
Eastern Cataract
Museum & Curios
Victoria Falls Town
Boiling Pot
Knife Edge
Border Post
ZIMBABWE
ZAMBIA
Batoka Plateau

The Victoria Falls, from every viewpoint, sunrise or sunset, presents a superlative photo opportunity.

Boiling Pot and Palm Grove

The Zambian side of Victoria Falls offers delights that cannot be found in Zimbabwe. From Zambia it's a steep but rewarding climb down through a belt of mopane and mukwa, where you'll find trees hung with colourful flowering vines or lianas with vividly descriptive names like Wild Grape, Old Man's Beard and Morning Glory. The **Palm Grove** itself is named after the wild date palm, or *Phoenix reclinata*, a 'reclining' tree whose trunk is typically tilted over.

Beyond the Grove is a river-fringing jumble of time-blackened rocks that vibrate subtly under your hands and feet as you crawl over them – the Falls are just around the corner. Climb as far as you can, going upstream, alongside the river's heavy flow, and you come to a chain bolted directly into the rock wall where the Zambian-side's rafting companies tie up in the morning and begin their rides in the **Boiling Pot**.

The Boiling Pot can appear deceptively and hypnotically calm in contrast to the wild spray storm of the mile-wide crashing water just above it. Here the Zambian and Zimbabwean sides of the river rejoin into a single, deep, churning, overwhelming, rock-tumbling current.

AGFA
PHOTO TIP

Do not leave film and equipment in vehicles or tents – the vehicle floor and the inside of a tent can get very hot. Keep your film as cool as possible, preferably in a coolbox or otherwise wrapped up.

QUOTABLE QUOTES
Australian visitor:
'It's a 360 degree bloody postcard.'
* Dr David Livingstone:
'Scenes so lovely must have been gazed upon by angels in their flight.'

ECOTRAILS

If you would like to experience the smaller creatures of the wild – the plants, flowers and so on – try Shearwater, Safari Par Excellence or Touch the Wild Safaris for unusual morning or afternoon ecotrails or tailor-made safaris.

SUN PROTECTION

Never underestimate the strength of the African sun. Use a minimum factor 15 sun block, wear a hat and avoid being out in the midday sun. Those with fair skin and red hair need to be particularly careful.

AGFA
PHOTO TIP

If you are travelling by plane, be aware that x-ray machines at the airport could possibly damage high speed film. As a precaution, pack film in a lead-lined bag.

GREAT AFRICAN STORIES

Cry the Beloved Country, Alan Paton
Flame Trees of Thika, Elsbeth Huxley
Out of Africa, Isak Dinesen
A Long Walk to Freedom, Nelson Mandela

The Batoka Plateau

From the Zambian side you can drive, walk or bicycle along the top of the **Batoka Plateau** to several spectacular viewpoints overlooking the rafting gorges below the Victoria Falls – views you cannot get to on the Zimbabwean side because of uncleared minefields left over from the bush war.

From the top you can take a steep, root-grabbing trail down to the river where the Tonga once fled to hide-out caves when the Ndebele warriors from the south came raiding. The caves are still used by Zambian fishermen who will stay by the river till they've caught, dried and smoked enough fish to take into Livingstone for sale.

At the apex of the Third and Fourth Gorge is a Zambian electrical power-generating station whose rail trolley ride down to the river was once something of a tourist attraction in the 1950s.

A few kilometres downstream from the Falls is a Stone Age archaeological site at the confluence of the Songwe and Zambezi rivers, but this is a four-wheel-drive-only trip as the plateau-top road beyond the power station becomes quite rough.

Knife Edge and the Eastern Cataract

The thin and precipitous wall of rock jutting out from the Zambian bank, along which a path has been cut, is known as **Knife Edge** and faces the silver-gold falls of the Eastern Cataract over which the sun rises.

The Knife Edge walk crosses over a pedestrian bridge with sweeping views of the Falls from the **Eastern Cataract** to a bowl-shaped depression on the lip called the **Armchair Falls**, and a magnificent view of the deceptively calm but treacherous **Boiling Pot** between Danger Point and Knife Edge. A Scandinavian government once offered to build a complete system of railings on the Knife Edge after one of its nationals fell over the side, but the Zambians opted to leave it as you will find it: slippery wet grass and rocks, woodlands and a precipitous drop over the edge.

Be wary of leaning over to get just the right picture; the Victoria Falls and the tempestuous Zambezi are seldom merciful. After the high river run of the rainy season has washed over the Falls, the once roaring, wall-wide

Danger Point faces Knife Edge in Zambia, with a continuous backdrop of thundering Falls.

46 HANDY GUIDE VICTORIA FALLS

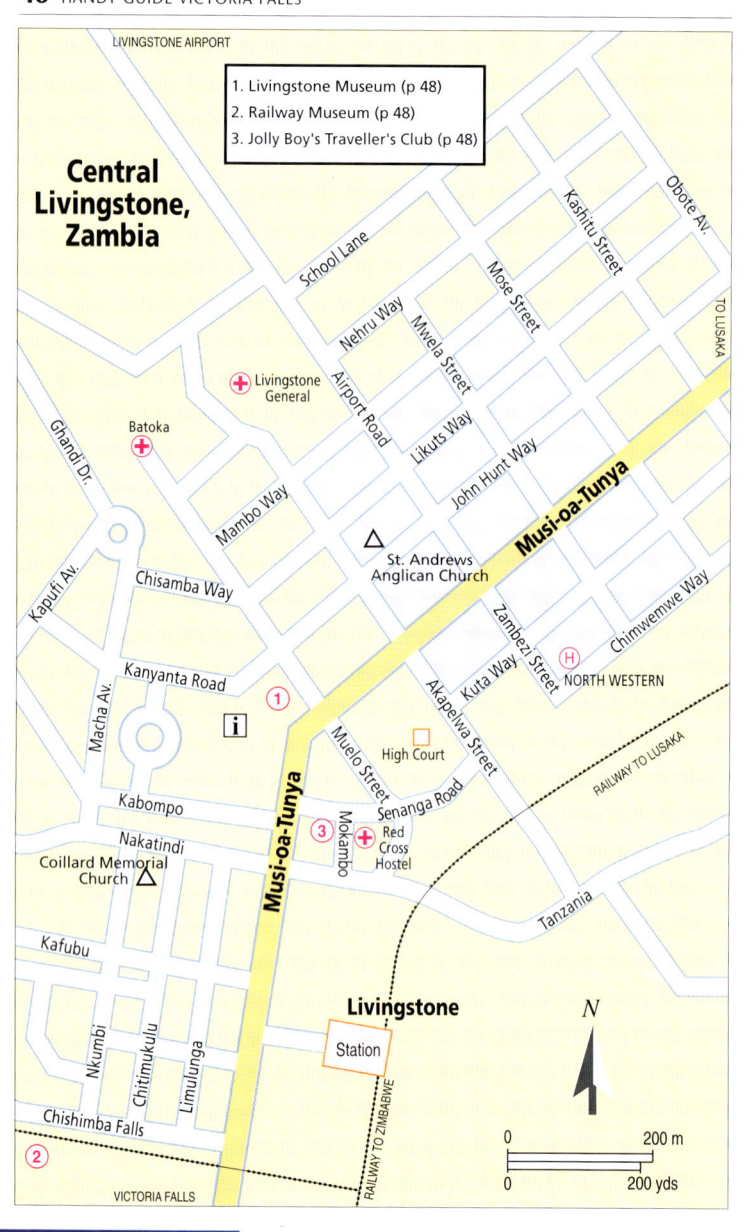

Central Livingstone, Zambia

1. Livingstone Museum (p 48)
2. Railway Museum (p 48)
3. Jolly Boy's Traveller's Club (p 48)

The royal sable antelope with its masked face and curved horns.

tide of the Eastern Cataract can dry up to only a thin ribbon of water. When this happens, you can walk out – only from the Zambian side – onto the upper lip of the Falls. Here you can explore a tidal pool-like rock shelf with lovely views of the upriver islands.

With hippos in the river and elephants swimming between the islands, bring along your binoculars, a bird book and a picnic basket. The sunsets over the river can be spectacular, and the feeling is memorable – being in such a peaceful place, and yet so close to the edge of one of the world's greatest waterfalls.

The Zambia National Tourist Board will provide you with more information; tel. (260) 3-321404.

En route to Livingstone

Off the main Musi-oa-Tunya Road to Livingstone is the **Maramba Cultural Centre**, a large grass boma where all-day traditional dancing takes place, attended by local people who will also get up and dance with the performers. Also off this main road is the **Royal Mile Boat Club** (no telephone number), the thatched **Luando Restaurant** at the Makumbi boat launch site with fish trap decor (no telephone number), and a river cruise boat dock. On Riverside Drive lies the **Mosi-oa-Tunya Zoological Park**, a 1,650-ha (4,078-acre) riverside National Park with a variety of game, including several white rhino, and incorporating the turn-of-the-century **Old Drift** river crossing and pioneer cemetery. The park is open from 06h00-18h00 and an entry fee is charged; tel. (260) 3-321396 for more details.

SABLE ANTELOPE

Only the gemsbok of Namibia can equal the majesty of the black-and-white **sable** with its long scimitar horns. Breeding males defend their territories during the rut with much bellowing, slashing and horn fencing – sometimes with bloody results. The Hwange and Zambezi national parks are particularly rich in sable.

AGFA PHOTO TIP

A 300-mm zoom lens is perfectly adequate for game photos, although a 400-mm focal length will be needed to shoot birds, especially if you are trying to capture birds skimming the water surface.

A WOMAN'S WORLD

At the shoulder, **elephant** males can stand up to 4 m (13 ft) high; the elephant world, however, is a matriarchal society in which the lead female in the family group rules. Groups consist of females and their young, which link with others to form herds. Males live in their own herds or alone.

GAME-VIEWING TIPS

* **Patience:** wait in one spot, don't always drive around.
* Be **quiet**.
* **Binoculars:** scan slowly and watch for movement.
* **Dress:** neutral khaki, hat, sunglasses and sunblock. Camouflage gear is not allowed.
* **Remember**, do not leave your car except at picnic sites or viewing platforms.

GAME DRIVES

Game drives are available from many safari operators. See the big animals such as lion, buffalo, elephant, hippo, zebra and giraffe. Try **Dabula Safaris** on tel./fax (263) 13-4453, 309 Parkway, Victoria Falls.

Livingstone

Livingstone was the first settlement at Victoria Falls and the country's capital till 1935. Most of the original buildings still stand, some barely, and it is rustic and romantic in a collapsed sort of way. You may not get black water fever these days but you shouldn't drink any tap water in Livingstone and also be wary of the fruit.

Livingstone has banks, safari companies, budget accommodation for backpackers, four churches and the **Jolly Boys Travellers' Club** in Maokambo Way (tel. [260] 3-321924). The **Railway Museum** in Chishimba Falls Road has not been able to prevent the rolling stock and engines from listing and rusting but they are still worth seeing, tel. (260) 3-321820. The museum is open 08h00-16h30 daily and an entrance fee is payable.

The **Livingstone Museum** (open daily) in the centre of town on Mosi-oa-Tunya Road, has relics, memorabilia, artefacts and old maps. It is open from 09h00-17h00 daily and an entry fee is charged; tel. (260) 3-321204 for further details.

Not far from the city are several **archaeological sites** covering man's long association with the Falls. To the north lie the magnificent game parks of Zambia, which include **Luangwa** and **Kafue**. Off the road are **Kubu Cabins**, tel. (260) 3-324093, and **Thorntree Tented Safari Camp**, tel. (260) 3-320823, and everyone's vision

Sindabezi Zambezi island camp, part of and 3km (2 miles) downstream of Tongabezi Lodge.

EXCURSIONS

Four-wheel-drive tours, one of many safaris offered at Victoria Falls.

of safari heaven, the riverside treehouse at **Tongabezi** where the food is so good, diners have actually applauded the chef; tel. (260) 3-323235.

Contact the Zambia National Tourist Board, tel. (260) 3-321404, for further details.

SAFARIS

Mobile four-wheel-drive safaris, hunting safaris, canoeing safaris, horse safaris and even elephant-back safaris are on offer at Victoria Falls, safari centre for the whole of northern Botswana, Zambia, Caprivi and Zimbabwe.

Walking safaris

Safari in Swahili means to walk, to adventure. The walking safari is the ultimate safari, an experience with the animals in the wild. A world of the silent predator, the sudden bird call warning, a dragonfly hovering over a water lily, a dungbeetle relentlessly pushing with its back legs, and tracking animals with bush experts who can explain the secrets of every tree and sound.

Walking safaris range from a gentle 1 km (just over half a mile) stroll, a 25 km (15 mile) power hike, to a 12-day swing through a circuit of national parks run by Leon Varley of Backpackers Africa. You can have everything carried for you, or you can carry your own backpack. The

---

VOICES OF THE NIGHT

It can be eerie listening to **hyaena** rev up a few hundred metres from your tent, but it is the quintessential call of the African night. Much maligned, these creatures are not cowards but rather powerful hunters. The young are born in holes in the ground. Hyaenas have jaws like a pressure-driven guillotine, and they are not averse to sampling a foot sticking out from under a tent flap!

AGFA PHOTO TIP

Run by hunter-guide, bush fundi and superb horsewoman Alison Baker, **horse trails**, lasting up to four days (half a day for novices) are quite special. There is an affinity between horse and game for, although trained to the saddle, the horse has not lost its instinctive awareness of movement and smell in the bush. Equally, a horse does not frighten game as people do, thus providing excellent photo opportunities. Rides depart from the Parkway-Courteney Selous stables near the Rainbow Hotel.; tel. (263) 13-4471.

50 HANDY GUIDE VICTORIA FALLS

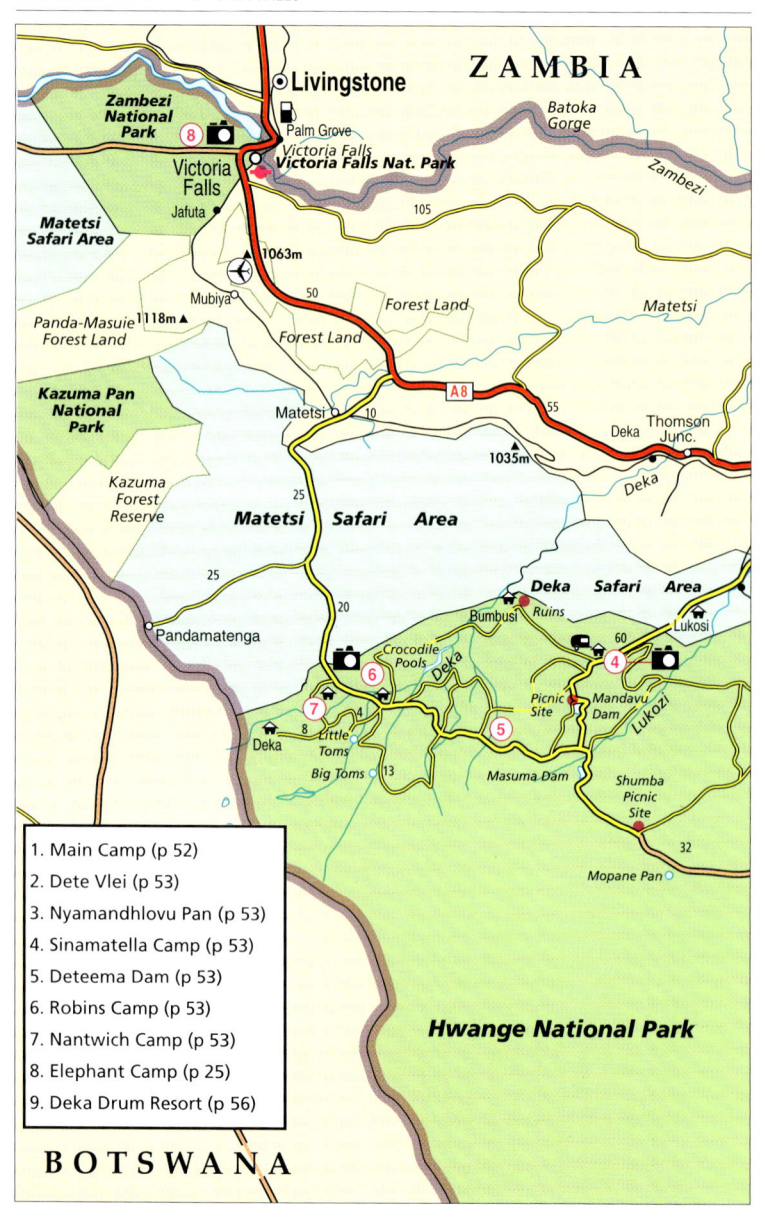

1. Main Camp (p 52)
2. Dete Vlei (p 53)
3. Nyamandhlovu Pan (p 53)
4. Sinamatella Camp (p 53)
5. Deteema Dam (p 53)
6. Robins Camp (p 53)
7. Nantwich Camp (p 53)
8. Elephant Camp (p 25)
9. Deka Drum Resort (p 56)

EXCURSIONS 51

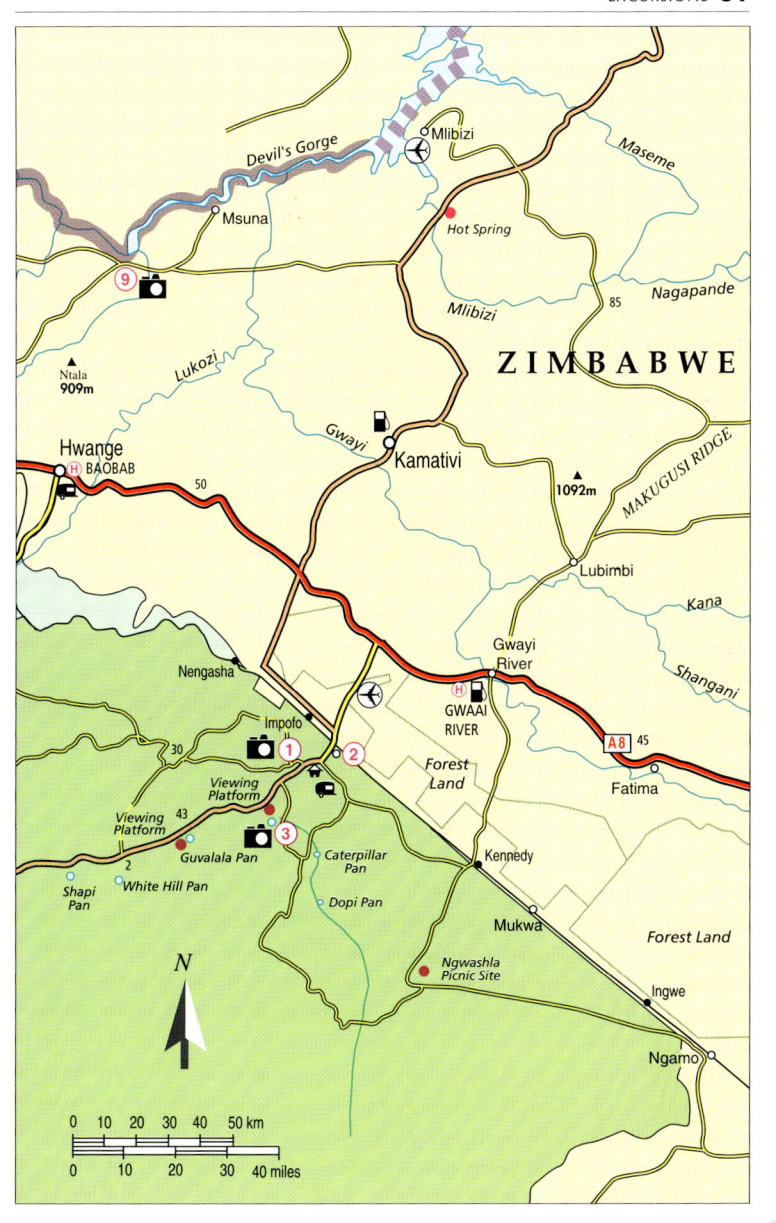

Elephants browse on the wide plains below Sinamatella's high cliffs.

AGFA PHOTO TIP

*Main Camp is renowned for its vast herds of **elephant** that come to drink at the many borehole-fed pans. **Hwange Safari Lodge** near Main Camp has its own waterhole and viewing platform, an ideal place to watch elephant drinking or taking a sand bath. These giant beasts fancy some 170 kg (375 pounds) of green fodder daily and at least 160 litres (35 gallons) of water. Vegetable ivory and marula fruit, together with camelthorn pods, are loved by them.*

memory that will remain when you return home may be of a klipspringer running with nimble grace across a sheer rock slope, or perhaps something delightfully absurd, like the sound of two elephants having a jazz trumpeting session. Consult the Advisory on page 63 for further details.

HWANGE NATIONAL PARK

Zimbabwe's largest game sanctuary, the 14,620 km^2 (5,645 mile^2) Hwange National Park, is home to some 107 different animals, including 3,000 zebra, 6,000 impala, 2,000 sable, 15,000 buffalo sometimes in herds 2,000 strong, and famously, 17,000 elephant, one of the last majestic herds on the continent. About 400 species of birds also live here in a multiplicity of habitats and trees that make the park a birder's delight.

The camps

Solar panels provide the electricity at the borehole-fed pans of **Main Camp**, one of three camps in the park. In the evening the elephant, in breeding herds of a hundred at a time, come down to drink at these pans.

The nearby 15-km-long (9.5 mile) **Dete Vlei** with its necklace of high trees is famous for its variety of game, while at the pans in southern Hwange, such as Kennedy One and Makwa, lion are regularly seen.

It's a day's game-viewing drive between Main and Sinamatella camps. **Sinamatella** is perched high on a cliff overlooking river, forest, ilala palms and vast plains. The best game spots in the vicinity are **Masuma, Mandavu** and **Deteema dams**. All the camps in Hwange have rustic chalets and good restaurants with gravel roads connecting them (the tar sections are potholed). **Robins-Nantwich** forms the third camp nearest the Falls, 116 km (72 miles) away. Nantwich has three olde-worlde chalets with outdoor wood boilers and bath, set high over a game-rich pan.

To reach Main Camp, turn off the main road 264 km (164 miles) from Bulawayo. Sinamatella Camp lies 40 km (25 miles) west of Hwange town. Robins and Nantwich camps can be reached by turning left off the Bulawayo road 390 km (242 miles) from that city and 48 km (30 miles) from Victoria Falls. It is then 68 km (42 miles) to Robins. Bookings can be made through National Parks Central Reservations; tel. 14-706077 Harare.

AGFA PHOTO TIP

The aloe-strewn rocky ridge of Sinamatella sits in splendid isolation high above an ancient flood plain with shimmering views worth capturing on film.

AGFA PHOTO TIP

Early mornings and late afternoons are the best times to view or photograph game as most animals lie up in the heat of the day. It's a good idea to wait at a waterhole, such as Main Camp's Nyamandhlovu Pan, for the game to come and drink, rather than driving around.

Giraffe and zebra seen from the game-viewing platform at Hwange's Nymandhlovu Pan.

54 HANDY GUIDE VICTORIA FALLS

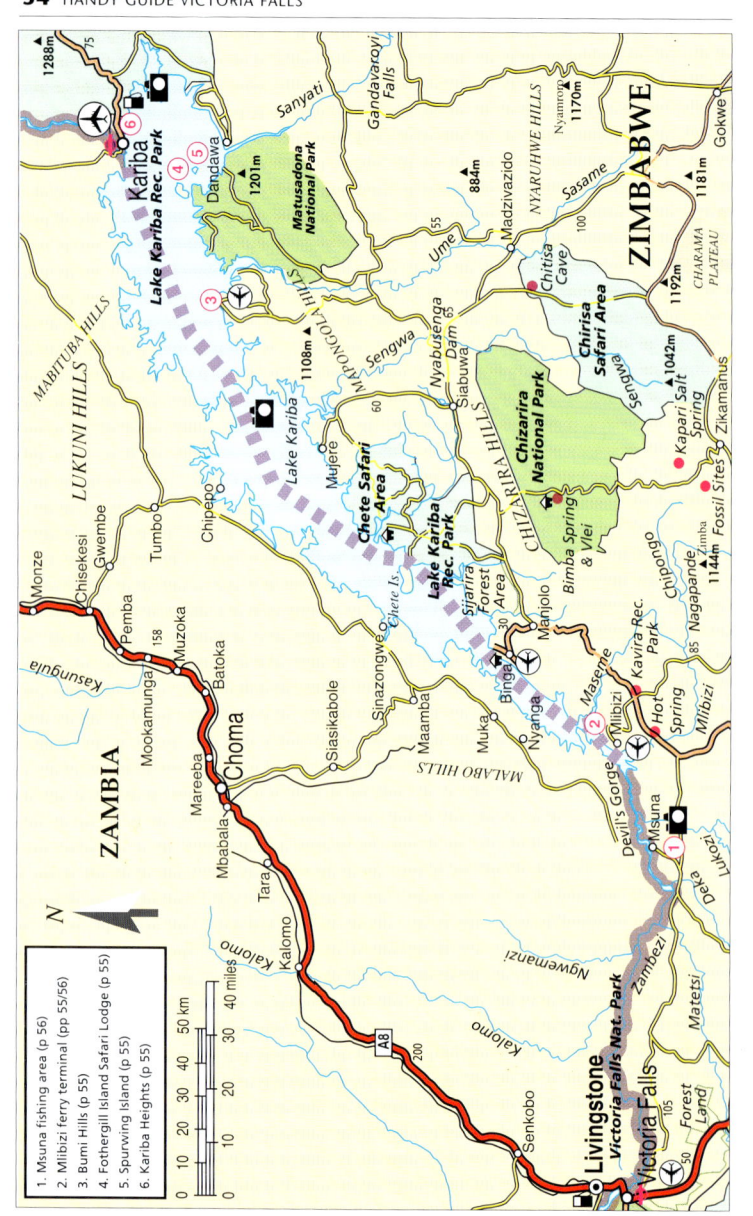

1. Msuna fishing area (p 56)
2. Milibizi ferry terminal (pp 55/56)
3. Bumi Hills (p 55)
4. Fothergill Island Safari Lodge (p 55)
5. Spurwing Island (p 55)
6. Kariba Heights (p 55)

KARIBA, THE GREAT LAKE

Visitors often combine a trip to Victoria Falls with a stay at Hwange and Kariba. They are often tempted to linger longer at Lake Kariba, a 282 km-long (175 miles) inland sea with safari islands, magnificent tiger fishing and green *Panicum* grass shores alive with buffalo, elephant and a wilderness of birds.

Kariba

Kariba's dam was completed in 1959. It soars 128 m (420 ft) high and is half a kilometre wide (¼ mile). Eighty-six Italian and Zimbabwean workers died in its construction, their names recorded in the coffer dam church atop **Kariba Heights village** where the views over the lake and Matusadona mountains are spectacular.

Visitors can opt for a three-day catamaran sail safari (tel. Harare on 14-335120), hire a houseboat (tel. Kariba on 161-2839) or luxuriate on the *Southern Belle*, a Mississippi-style river boat (tel. 14-794377). Get to one of the safari islands if you can – **Fothergill** (tel. 161-2253/2378), **Bumi Hills** (tel. 161-2353) or **Spurwing** (tel. 161-2466). All offer big game, drumbeat meals and stars at night – the complete African experience.

AGFA
PHOTO TIP
The best views of **Lake Kariba** are from the summit at Kariba Heights village.

KARIBA FERRY
An exciting way to get from Harare to Victoria Falls is to go on the **Kariba overnight car ferry** to Mlibizi. The 282 km long journey (175 miles) along the length of the lake takes 22 hours, all meals are provided as well as reclining chairs for the night on deck or in the saloon. From Mlibizi it is only about 250 km (160 miles) on tarred roads to the Falls.

A boat safari from Fothergill Island Safari Lodge gives close-up game-viewing opportunities.

AGFA
PHOTO TIP

*The spiritual home of the tigerfish is how **Deka Drum fishing resort** bills itself. Sited on the Zambezi an hour's drive from both Mlibizi and Hwange town, it has magnificent riverine vistas and many hippo.*

The world's largest freshwater angling competition for tigerfish is held annually in October at Kariba, when the temperatures can reach 55 °C (130 °F). Commercial fishing is based on *kapenta* and these sardines are widely used as bait for catching tigerfish.

For serious students of the wild, visit Kuburi Wilderness near Kariba village (tel. 161-2538), while the most relaxing way to get to the Falls is on the overnight Kariba car ferry journey; tel. Kariba Ferries on 14-614162/7 for more information and see boxes on pp 55 and 59.

EN ROUTE TO VICTORIA FALLS

From Kariba

Mlibizi is a fishing and birding resort at the headwaters of Lake Kariba, where the Zambezi leaves Devil's Gorge. Turn right at the crossroads 281 km (175 miles) from Bulawayo. It is then 95 km (60 miles) to Mlibizi on a good metal road.

The Mlibizi Basin is an area of attractive, thickly-wooded bays, gorges and islands and where the lake broadens up to 2 km wide (1.25 miles) in parts. It is a uniquely tranquil holiday lagoon, specializing in tigerfishing, and hires out fishing boats, canoes and rafts.

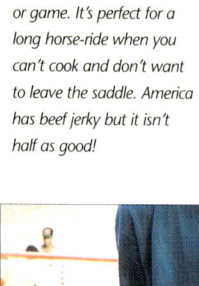

BILTONG

Biltong is a spiced, dried meat made from beef or game. It's perfect for a long horse-ride when you can't cook and don't want to leave the saddle. America has beef jerky but it isn't half as good!

The thatched Mlibizi Hotel (tel. 151-271) has bungalows among the lakeshore trees, shady green lawns, swimming pool, patio dining and two lakeshore pubs. The area is far from the madding crowd and the overnight ferry to Kariba begins its 22-hour-long journey here. Mlibizi can be very hot in summer.

From Hwange

Deka Drum Fishing Resort on the Zambezi River has furnished cabins for hire – tel. 181-250524. Turn right off the road from Bulawayo at Hwange town and drive for 50 km (30 miles) on a tar road. **Msuna fishing camp**, popular with Bulawayo anglers, is a little further on.

The tigerfish is the prized sport trophy in Zimbabwe.

Queen of the lake, the Southern Belle *sails out of the pages of Mark Twain.*

From Bulawayo

Bulawayo, the Ndebele-Zulu 'place of slaughter', has many old colonial buildings. Other places worth seeing in the city are the **Natural History Museum** (which has 75 000 animal species in scenic wildlife settings, the largest in the southern hemisphere), the **Railway**

Displayed against a backdrop of lake and sky are these sculptures at Kariba Heights.

BLACK EAGLES
The *Matobo Hills* are believed to contain Africa's greatest concentration of the magnificent black eagle (Aquila verreauxii), found only in this type of mountainous country. They feed on dassies (hyraxes), which live among the rocks.

AGFA
PHOTO TIP
The beautiful **Naletale ruins**, an hour and a half's drive from Bulawayo, are noted for their intricate herringbone, chequered and chevron patterns carved into the stonework. Naletale was built 300 years ago.

Museum, the **Chipangali Wildlife Orphanage**, the acclaimed **Amakhosi dance troupe**, the **Mzilikazi Craft Centre** and nearby **Kame Ruins**, second only in importance to Great Zimbabwe.

If passing through Bulawayo, don't miss the chaotic, weather-cracked hills of the **Matobos**, the ancestral spirit land of the Rozvi mediums, 45 km (28 miles) south of Bulawayo. The *amatobo*, or bald-headed hills as Zulu warlord Mzilikazi called them, is a moonscape of endless granite humpbacks. **Cecil Rhodes** called the Matobos 'one of the world's views'. He is buried here on a bare granite hill in an amphitheatre of giant balls of stone, with a plain bronze inscription hewed into the ground. Hundreds of San 'Bushmen' rock paintings are found in the many caves of the Matobos.

If you are travelling from Bulawayo by road, stop roughly halfway at the **Gwaai River Hotel**, an eccentric hunters' haunt full of character and characters. Guests are encouraged to bring their own musical instruments on pub nights (every night). The hotel is situated 248 km (154 miles) from Bulawayo, tel. 118-355.

From Beitbridge

Sentinel Limpopo Safaris has a luxury private estate of 32,773 ha (81,000 acres) near the Sashe-Limpopo confluence, some 80 km (50 miles) west of Beitbridge. Dinosaur sites, rock art and horseback game-viewing are on offer. Access is on gravel roads or via Inter-Air from Johannesburg to nearby Messina. Tel./fax 186-351, P O Box 36, Beitbridge.

From Namibia or Botswana

If you are arriving from Namibia or Botswana, the village of **Katima Mulilo**, capital of the Caprivi Strip on the Zambezi, is a comfortable and pretty riverside stopover, 200 km (125 miles or four immigration posts) from Victoria Falls, mainly on rough gravel roads.

Brightly coloured lizards bask on the Matobo's warm rocks.

The Matobos, Kipling's 'granite of the ancient north. Great spaces washed by the sun.'

VISITOR'S DIGEST

GETTING THERE

By Air
There are direct flights to Victoria Falls from Harare, Bulawayo, Cape Town and Johannesburg. Regular airport buses leave from Victoria Falls airport, and some hotels also offer this service. Internal flights to the main visitor destinations are operated by **Air Zimbabwe**, tel. (263) 13-4316/4518 and **Zimbabwe Express Airlines**, tel. (263) 4-729681. Air charter companies include **Executive Air**, tel. (263) 4-302248, **United Air**, tel. (263) 4-575016/731715, and **Air Tabex**, tel. (263) 4-790225. Flight enquiries: tel. Victoria Falls (263) 13-4250. **Livingstone Airport**, Zambia, tel. (260) 3-321153.

There are no banking facilities at the airport but **Barclays**, **Standard Chartered** and **Zimbank** have offices in the village. Car hire available from the airport includes **Europcar**, **Avis** and **Hertz**. There is a US$20 departure tax (US$50 and US$100 notes not accepted) if you are leaving Zimbabwe from Victoria Falls.

By Road
A superb road network connects Zimbabwe with all its neighbours. Internally all the major visitor centres are connected by good tar roads. Beware of game at night, cattle, and some rather poor driving. On entering the country, you will need to produce a police clearance certificate, your vehicle registration and vehicle insurance; check with the AA before departure. In Zimbabwe one drives on the left and gives way to the right.

By Rail
Zimbabwe is linked by rail with its neighbours South Africa, Zambia, Botswana and Mozambique. There is a daily train from Bulawayo to Victoria Falls, tel. (263) 13-4391, as well as twice-monthly steam train safaris from Bulawayo via Hwange; tel. **Rail Safaris**, (263) 9-75575. The Victoria Falls station is opposite the Victoria Falls Hotel in Mellet Drive, tel. (263) 13-4391.

GETTING AROUND

Car Hire
Hire a car from **Europcar**, tel. (263) 13-4598/4344; **Avis**, tel. (263) 13-4532; **Hertz**, tel. (263) 13-4267 or in Zambia, **Eagle Travel**, tel. (260) 3-320129/320120.

Town Travel
The best way to tour the Falls is by hired bicycle, tel. (263) 13-4348 or 4424, by scooter, tel. (263) 13-4402, on foot, or by the **Victoria Falls Rambler**, a tractor-pulled trailer that tours the village. Or catch a UTC or hotel bus. Check at any hotel for details on the above. For taxis tel. (263) 13-4743. For a one-day tour of Livingstone, contact **Makora Quest**, tel. (260) 3-321679.

Coach Services
Coach services link the main Zimbabwe centres. **Blue Arrow** (United Transport Group) operates a weekly trip to Victoria Falls; tel. Harare on (263) 4-729514, fax. (263) 4-729572, or Bulawayo on (263) 9-65548, fax. (263) 9-65549.

GENERAL INFORMATION

Climate
Victoria Falls is hot for most of the year. In winter (June and July) the days are warm, but cool at night. November brings the rain. The flow of the Falls is lowest in November and December; the end of the rains from February and March onwards see the heaviest flow and volume of spray.

Electricity
The power system is 220 volts AC; US appliances require an adaptor. Plugs are usually 13-amp square pins.

Health Hazards
Malaria prophylactics should be taken at the Victoria Falls and if travelling beyond Harare, Bulawayo or the Eastern Highlands. The tap drinking water is perfectly safe. Aids is a major disease in Zimbabwe. Beware of sunburn; use a Factor 15 plus cream and always

wear a hat. Wild animals roam around Victoria Falls, although seldom seen in town. It is advisable to travel by car at night.

Measurement
Zimbabwe uses the metric system.

Medical services
There are private doctors in Victoria Falls. Contact Pumula Pharmacy for details, tel. (263) 13-4403. Government clinics are available in Chinotimba high-density suburb. The nearest large hospital is in Bulawayo. In an emergency in either Zimbabwe or Zambia, contact Medical Air Rescue Service (MARS), tel. (263) 13-4764/4646, or for a private doctor, tel. (263) 13-3356/423121.

Money
Currency Exchange: Foreign currency can be exchanged at banks and hotels. There are no restrictions on the amount of traveller's cheques or foreign cash visitors can bring in or take out of the country. International credit cards are acceptable, particularly at hotels and restaurants.
Tipping: Tips at around 10% are much appreciated in most situations.

Newspapers
A Guide to Victoria Falls is a local paper which is published regularly by Safari Travel Agency, tel. (263) 13-4571. All the Harare papers, such as *The Herald* and *Financial Gazette*, are available at Victoria Falls.

Security
Petty theft does occur. Crime and theft is widespread in Livingstone, so guard your belongings, car and cash. Remember that a visible money belt identifies you as a visitor. In Zimbabwe, possession of drugs, including cannabis, is a punishable offence.

Telecommunications
STD dialling is possible to anywhere in the world from Zimbabwe. To dial out, dial 110 to obtain the international satellite, then 44 (UK), 1 (USA and Canada), 27 (South Africa) or 61 (Australia), followed by the number. The dialling code to reach Zimbabwe is 263. Add an extra '1' before local telephone codes when dialing within Zimbabwe.

In Zimbabwe every exchange has its own dialling code. Where dashes occur in this code, it is an indication that you should wait for a further dialling tone before dialling the main number. To obtain operator assistance for local calls, dial 0. There are public call boxes in most of the main centres.

Fax facilities are widely available; many organizations in resort areas still have telex as an option, and a few are using E-mail.

Time
Zimbabwe is two hours ahead of Greenwich Mean (or Universal Standard) Time, one hour ahead of Central European Winter Time and seven hours ahead of the USA's Eastern Standard Winter Time. Sydney is eight hours ahead of Zimbabwe.

Tourist Information
Regional publicity associations include:
* Victoria Falls Publicity Association, tel. (263) 13-4202.
* Zambia National Tourist Board, tel. (260) 3-321404, fax. (260) 3-321487.
* Harare Publicity Bureau, tel. (263) 4-705085/6/7.
* Bulawayo, tel. (263) 9-60867.
* Mutare, tel. (263) 20-64711.
* Masvingo, tel. (263) 39-62643.

Trading hours
Banks are open weekdays 08h00-15h00 (Wednesdays half-day closing at 13h00) and on Saturdays 08h00-11h30.
Post offices are open weekdays 08h00-16h30 and 08h00-11h30 on Saturdays.
Shops are usually open weekdays 08h00-17h00, and 08h00-13h00 on Saturdays.

WHERE TO STAY

Luxury Hotels
Victoria Falls
A'Zambezi River Lodge, riverside location; tel. (263) 13-4561, fax. (263) 13-4536.
Elephant Camp, for elephant back safaris,

15 km (9.5 miles) southwest of Victoria Falls on border of Zambezi National Park; tel. (263) 13-2004/4219, fax. (263) 13-4349.
Elephant Hills, golf course and conference hotel, call the Zimbabwe Sun Group; tel. (263) 13-4793, fax. (263) 13-4655.
Ilala Lodge, centrally situated; tel. (263) 13-4737/6, fax. (263) 13-4417.
Imbabala Safari Camp, riverside chalets near Kazangula and Caprivi, some 70 km (45 miles) from Victoria Falls; tel. (263) 13-2004/4219, fax. (263) 13-4349.
Masuwe Lodge, tent and thatch safari lodge near the Zambezi National Park, 9 km (5.5 miles) from the Falls with game-viewing platform overlooking floodlit water hole; tel. (263) 13-426512, fax. (263) 4-750785.
Matetsi Private Game Reserve 49,000ha (121 107 acres) and 18 km (11 miles) of river frontage. Contact Corporation Africa on Johannesburg line; tel. (27) 11-8038421, fax (27) 11-8031810.
Sizinda Lodge, hilltop wilderness chalets, 42 km (26 miles) south of Victoria Falls; tel. Bushveld Safaris (263) 4-727080, fax. (263) 4-796432.
Victoria Falls Hotel, famous old hotel, contact the Zimbabwe Sun Group; tel. (263) 13-4203, fax. (263) 13-4586.
Victoria Falls Safari Lodge, big thatched complex overlooking game pan and bush, 4 km (2.5 miles) from the Falls; tel. (263) 13-3201, fax. (263) 13-3205.

Livingstone (Zambia)
Kubu Cabins, located on the Zambezi River, open year round; tel. (260) 3-324093, fax. (260) 3-324091.
Musi-oa-Tunya Intercontinental Hotel, the closest hotel to the Victoria Falls; tel. (260) 3-321210/11, fax. (260) 3-321128.
Rainbow Lodge, rondavels on the Zambezi River, 1 km (2/8 mile) from the border; tel. (260) 3-321806/8, fax. (260) 3-320236.
Thorn Tree Tented Safari Camp, situated on the Zambezi River and open all year; tel. (260) 3-320823, fax. (260) 3-320277.
Tongabezi, luxurious safari lodge constructed over the river, open year round; tel. (119) 3-323235, fax. (119) 3-323224.

Wasawange Lodge, Airport Road; chalets and rooms, tel. (260) 3-324066, fax. (260) 3-324067.

Budget accommodation
Victoria Falls
National Parks lodges and nine game-viewing and fishing camps; write well in advance to National Parks, P O Box CY826, Causeway, Harare; tel. (263) 4-706077 or call Victoria Falls on (263) 13-4222.
Town Council Rest Camp, town centre, chalets, camping and caravaning; tel. (263) 13-4210, fax. (263) 13-4308.

Livingstone
Red Cross Hotel, the best in Livingstone, clean and inexpensive. Mokambo Road; tel. (260) 3-322473.
Rainbow Lodge Campsite, only 1 km (just over half a mile) from the border post and 9 km (5.5 miles) from the centre of Livingstone; tel. (260) 3-321806. Beware of campsite theft.

WHERE TO EAT

Victoria Falls
All hotels have one or more restaurants with an à la carte menu.
Boma Restaurant at Victoria Falls Safari Lodge, open-air dining of game meat and potjiekos (layered stew cooked in cast iron three-legged pot); tel. (263) 13-3201.
Explorers, Sopers Centre, pub food, live music, river rafters rave-up spot; tel. (263) 13-4298.
Ilala Lodge, restaurant has good vegetarian meals; tel. (263) 13-4736.
Livingstone Room at Victoria Falls Hotel, elegant dining; hotel also offers evening patio buffet barbecue; tel. (263) 13-4203.
Naran's Take-Aways, Sopers Centre, Indian food; tel. (263) 13-4425.
The Cattleman, Pumula Mall, good steakhouse; tel. (263) 13-4767.
The Pizza Bistro, Sopers Centre, small, cosy, good pasta and pizzas; tel. (263) 13-4396.
Wimpy, breakfasts and burgers, corner Parkway/Livingstone Way; tel. (263) 13-4470.

Livingstone

There are restaurants at all the big hotels and lodges (*see accommodation on pp 60/61*) but apart from those, the choice is not great. Try:

Luando, located at the Makumbi boat launch site; no telephone number.

Mukombo Restaurant, one block behind Main Street. Zairese music.

TOURS AND EXCURSIONS

Bungi-jumping, *African Extreme*, c/o Shearwater; tel. (263) 13-4471, *Valley Ventures*, Livingstone; tel. (260) 3-320742, or book at the bridge.

Canoeing, upper Zambezi above the Falls, try *Safari Par Excellence*, tel. (263) 13-4424, fax. (263) 13-4510. *The Zambezi Canoe Company*, tel. (263) 13-4298, fax. (263) 13 4683. *Shearwater*, tel. (263) 13-4471, fax. (263) 13-4341. *Kandahar Safaris*, tel. (263) 13-4502, fax. (263) 13-4556. *Frontiers*, tel. (263) 13-4772.

Crocodile Ranch (Zambezi Nature Sanctuary); tel. (263) 13-4637.

Elephant Back Safaris tel. (263) 13-2004, fax. (263) 13-4349.

Flight of Angels, aircraft and helicopter flips. *United Air*, tel. (263) 13-4530. *Southern Cross Aviation*, tel. (263) 13-4453. Microlight flights: c/o *Batoka Sky* (263) 13-4424.

Game-viewing, try any Victoria Falls safari operator (at least 30 at Victoria Falls).

Golf, Elephant Hills Hotel; tel. (263) 13-4503/4793.

Horse trails, *Zambezi Horse Trails*, tel. (263) 13-4471.

Local culture tours, *Touch the Wild*, tel. (263) 13-4694, fax. (263) 13-4676.

Night drives, game-viewing; tel. (263) 13-4614, fax. (263) 13-4614.

River cruising, *Mosi-oa-Tunya Cruises*, tel. (263) 13-4780. *UTC*, tel. (263) 13-4267. *Zambezi River Cruises*, tel. (263) 13-4637. *Safari par Excellence*, tel. (263) 13-4424. *Abercrombie and Kent*, tel. (263) 13-5800.

Seaplane, converted Cessna 185; tel. (263) 13-3300, fax. (263) 13-3299.

Skydiving, *Zambezi Vultures*, tel. (263) 13-4424.

Traditional dancing at the *Falls Craft Village* or *Victoria Falls Hotel*, tel. (263) 13-4309.

Walking safaris, *Back Packers Africa*, tel. (263) 13-4424, fax. (263) 13-4510. *Khangela Safaris*, tel. (263) 13-4502, fax. (263) 13-4556.

White-water rafting, *Shearwater*, tel. (263) 13-4471, fax. (263) 13-4341. *Safari Par Excellence*, tel. (263) 13-4424, fax. (263) 13-4510. *Frontiers*, tel. (263) 13-5800, fax. (263) 13-5801; *Sobek*, tel. Livingstone (260) 3-321432, fax. (260) 3-323542, and Victoria Falls, tel. (263) 13-2069.

Zambezi Wine Route, *Zambezi Canoe and Safari Co*, tel. (263) 13-2059, fax. (263) 13-2058.

Deeper into Zambia

Luangwa Valley and Kafue National Park, *Sobek Adventures*, tel. (260) 1-224248. fax. (260) 1-224265.

Zambia safaris and canoeing, *Makora Quest*, tel. (260) 3-321679 (Off); 320400 (Res). fax. (260) 3-320732.

USEFUL CONTACT NUMBERS

AA: tel. (263) 13-4764.
Air Zimbabwe: tel. (263) 13-4518/4316 (4255 is the airport).
Ambulance: tel. (263) 13-4692/3.
Doctor: tel. (263) 13-3356/423121.
Fire brigade: tel. (263) 13-4337.
Hospital: tel. (263) 13-4692/3.
Locksmith: no locksmith but try *Fawcett Security*, tel. (263) 13-4770.
Medical Air Rescue Service (MARS): tel. (263) 13-4764/4646 (in Victoria Falls ring only 4764/4646); in Livingstone area as well.
Museum (Zambia): Musi-o-Tunya Road, 09h00-17h00 daily, tel. (260) 3-321204.
National Parks: Central Reservations, Harare, tel. (263) 4-706077, or call Victoria Falls on (263) 13-4222.
Pharmacy: Pumula Centre, tel. (263) 13-4403; *Zambia:* (260) 3-321640/321980.
Police (Emergency): 99; *Livingstone:* 999.
Samaritan Service: tel. Bulawayo (263) 9-65000 or Harare (23) 4-722000.
Visa enquiries: tel.. (263) 13-4237.

INDEX

Page numbers in *italics* indicate photographs.

Airport tax 7
Armchair Falls 44
Around and about Victoria Falls 26-29

Baines, Thomas 5
Batoka Gorge 4, 13, *32*, *33*, 34
Batoka Plateau 44
bicycle hire 22
Big Tree 18, *18*
bird trails 27
bird-watching 13
Boiling Pot 6, 43, 44
Bulawayo 19, 39, 53, 56, 58
bungi-jumping 31, 33, *33*

Campfire Project 41
camping 20
canoeing and kayaking 36, *36*, *37*
car hire 17
Cataract Island 7
Chain Walk 6, 7, 14
Chamabonda Drive 20, 29
Chapel of St Mary Magdalene 19
Coillard, François 12, 35
Courteney Selous Crescent 4, 16, 17
Crocodile Ranch 27, 28, *28*, 38
Curio Row *16*, 21

Dam
  Deteema (Hwange) 53
  Kariba 55
  Mandavu (Hwange) 53
  Masuma (Hwange) 53
Danger Point 6, 12, 13, 31, 44, *45*
Deka Drum Fishing Resort 56
Dete Vlei 53
Devil's Cataract 4, 6, *6*, 7, 13, 14
Devil's Gorge 34, 56

Eagles
  black 58
  fish 33
Eastern Bank 39
Eastern Cataract 39, 44, 47
ecotrails 44
Elephant Camp 25, *25*
Excursions 38-59

Falcon, taita 33
Falls Craft Village 4, 16, 17, 20, 21, *21*, 22, *22*
fishing and camping sites 28, 31

Gambling 25
Elephant Hills Hotel 26, 27
Makasa Sun Casino Hotel 25
game lodges and pans 29

History 5
Horseshoe Falls 6
horse trails 49
Hotel
  A'Zambezi 11, 18, 23, 24
  Elephant Hills 24, 25, 26, *26*
  Makasa Sun Casino 11, 23, 25
  Mlibizi 56
  Mosi-oa-Tunya Intercontinental, Zambia 24, 39
  Rainbow 23
  Sprayview 23
  Victoria Falls 4, 5, 17, 18, *18*, 19, *19*, 20, 21, 24, 31, 34
hunting safaris 41
Hwange camps
  Main 52
  Nantwich 53
  Robins 53
  Sinamatella *52*, 53

Information Bureau 16
Introduction 4

Kalai Island 41
Kariba ferry 55
Kariba Heights 55, *57*
Kazangula 36, 39
Knife Edge 39, 44, *45*
Kuburi Wilderness 56

Lake Kariba 30, 33, 35, *55*, 55, 56, 57, 58
language 26
Livingstone, Dr David 5, 7, 29, 41, 43
Livingstone Island 6, 39, 41
Livingstone's statue 6, *6*, 7, 14
Livingstone Way 16, 17, 20, 22, 29
Livingstone, Zambia 16, 19, 47, 48
Lodge
  Ilala Lodge 23, *23*
  Rainbow, Zambia 24
  Victoria Falls Safari 23
  Tongabezi, Zambia 41, *48*, 49

Main Falls 4, 6, 10, 11, *10/11*, 43
malaria 27
Matetsi Game Reserve 29, 39
Matetsi Safari Area 28
Matobo Hills 58, *59*
Mlibizi 35, 55, 58
Moffat
  Robert 7
  Mary 7
mosi-oa-tunya 4, 12
Mpala Jena 28, 31
Msuna fishing area 56
Msuna River 34

Naletale Ruins 58
National Park 28, 29, 53
  Hwange 38, 47, 52, *52*, 53, *53*, 55, 56
  Victoria Falls 5, 6, 16
  Zambezi 16, 17, 20, 23, 26, 28, 29
  Nyamandhlovu Pan, Hwange *53*

Old Drift 5, 16, 47

Palm Grove 39, 43
Parkway 16, 17, 22, 26, 28, 29

Rail safaris 38
railway station 16, 19
Rainbow Falls 6, 12
Rain Forest 4, 6, 14-15, *15*, 18
Rhodes, Cecil John 30, 31, 58
river cruises 37, *37*
robin, Heuglin's 14, *15*

Sadza 24
safaris 49, *49*
Selous, Frederick Courteney 5
scooter hire 17
Siamunungu 28
sky safaris 38, *38*, 39
Smith, Ian 25
Soper, Jack 30, 33
Southern Belle 55, *57*
Spencer, Terry 38
Stanley, Sir Henry Morton 5
swimming pools 11

Tigerfish 56, *56*
traditional dancing 19, 20, *20*, 21

Victoria Falls 4, 6-13, *12*, 14, 37, 38, 39, 41, 43, 44, 47, 53, 55
statistics 10
Victoria Falls Bridge, 4, 14, 19, 30, 31, *30/31*, 33, 34
Victoria Falls Town 16-25
Visitor's Digest 60-63

Waterfalls 4
white-water rafting 34, *34*, 35, *35*, 36
wildlife 29
  buffalo 37
  cheetah 29
  crocodile 27, 28, *28*
  elephant 47, 52, *52*
  hippos 41, *41*
  hyaena 49
  lizard 58
  sable antelope 47, *47*
  vervet monkey 14, *14*
  warthog 27
wining and dining 22
wood carvings 13, *13*

Zambezi Drive 18
Zambezi Nature Sanctuary *see* Crocodile Ranch
Zambezi River 4, 6, 7, 10, 13, 18, 23, 24, 26, 30-38, 39, 44, 58, 56
Zambezi River Festival 35, 36
Zambia 6, 16, 24, 31, 38, 39, 41, 43, 44, 47, 48, 49